Insights from
The Secret Teachings of Jesus:
The Gospel of Thomas

Christan Amundsen, MTh, MA

Sunstar
PUBLISHING LTD.

Insights from
The Secret Teachings of Jesus:
The Gospel of Thomas

United States Copyright, 1998
© Christan Amundsen, MTh, MA

Sunstar Publishing, Ltd.
204 South 20th Street
Fairfield, Iowa 52556

Cover Design: Amanda Collett
Formatting: Sharon A. Dunn

LCCN: 98-89351
ISBN: 1-887472-57-6

Readers interested in obtaining further
information on the subject matter of this
book are invited to correspond with:

The Secretary, Sunstar Publishing, Ltd.
204 South 20th Street, Fairfield, Iowa 52556

More Sunstar Books at *www.newagepage.com*

Table of Contents

Foreword

Recently discovered in Upper Egypt, the Gospel of Thomas, most scholars agree, is an authentic early list of "secret sayings" attributed to Jesus. Each of the 114 sayings is a kind of koan, a cryptic aphorism that invites – requires – reflection to disclose its meaning. According to the first saying the reward for undertaking this difficult task is great: it offers the possibility of overcoming death, and awakening spiritual life.

This commentary by Christan Amundsen is a remarkable one: it offers insights from the heart and mind of a man who has dared accept this gospel's difficult challenge – to renounce what the world believes it can offer of power, authority, wealth, and happiness, to embrace the arduous and often solitary path of spiritual inquiry. This gives him insights not available to those whose relationship to the Gospel of Thomas is merely scholarly or curious. His understanding of Insight 97, for example, is astonishingly apt and persuasive, and wholly unlike what anyone else I know has said about this puzzling parable. What I find moving in this work is the self-honesty, the humor, and the depth of spiritual path. For all of what he gives us here, we are in his debt.

– Elaine Pagels
Harrington Spear Paine Professor of Religion,
Princeton University
Author, *The Gnostic Gospels*
January 19, 1999

Introduction

Years ago when I first read the Gospel of Thomas I was captivated by its language and depth. Not like the other Gospels, it is a collection of sayings one after the other in rapid fire motion. Each saying has an edge – a way of driving to something within that is uncommon. Some of the sayings appear in the traditional New Testament, while others stand alone within this text. The dating of the document is variously given depending upon the scholar doing the dating. I have seen it dated as early as the first century to as late as the fourth. Likewise, its origin is not well established. Some say it is an alternate document within early Christianity, while others ascribe this text to the Manichaeans, a rival religious sect to Christianity. This debate may or may not matter to the reader. It may matter since the text itself leads one to call into question the essence of Christianity – if the document is viewed as coming from the early Christian community or from Christ himself. This is so since no mention is made of the significance of Jesus' death on the cross or his resurrection. Furthermore, no reference is given to what he did or did not do with regard to miracles, presumably because these items are contrary to the essence of the teachings, namely that inner awakening is the important point of spirituality, not material evidence or the wonderment of supernatural events within history. All this is to say that the Gospel of Thomas, if it is a document of the early Christian Church or from Christ himself, certainly speaks of a different kind of Christianity than has been passed down from the "Church Fathers" who seemed to have a great deal more invested in the creation and sustaining of an organized church body than in imparting a liberating message of spirituality.

On the other hand, the issue of origin may not be important to the reader, because after all truth is truth regardless of its context and origin. Whether it comes from the earliest Christians, as I suspect it does, or it simply reflects a great wisdom being imparted years later by heretics of orthodox religion, begs the real question. The essential issue when one reads this beautiful text is whether it speaks to the heart of truth or not. If one can, for the moment of reading, suspend all preconceived notions as to the issues surrounding the text and simply let the text speak – it is my sense one will find it filled with wisdom and truth of an extraordinary nature. For unlike many ancient texts, it has a modern appeal of psychological significance that cannot be overlooked. It is at once both existential and relevant to everyday life, and yet evokes in one a deeper sense of another reality pressing in upon the very soul of the reader.

I have attempted to liberate the heart of the text from the literal word by word translation that is common. Without taking liberties with the essential thoughts, I have tried to let the words live and breath as I think they were meant. When read this way, they come alive in the heart and awaken the soul to something beyond itself – a divine spark that slumbers without this calling. The text itself suggests that in its very reading and understanding, true life is to be found, a kind of wake-up call to the Spirit. If we are to read this text not just with our eyes, but with our soul as well, then perhaps that wake-up call can ring through.

The frame of reference of the content of this Gospel is the "secret sayings" of Jesus. They are secret in the sense that they are the private or personal teachings of Jesus. It should not astound us that Jesus would have spoken more directly and on a different level to those who were closest to him. His public message was meant to be just that – public, and for general consumption. The public teachings would by their very nature be less substantial and merely a beginning into something far richer. Those closest to Jesus, and those who desired to push deeper into the essence of spirituality, were given greater detail and harder lessons.

Because the teachings in the Gospel of Thomas are non-authoritarian and introspective, the early church could not use it to form a church around. The Gospel of Thomas requires people to seek within themselves, and not be blinded by collective religiosity – exactly the opposite of what the Church Fathers needed to start a church. However, once people became thirsty for more, the public Gospels were less than fulfilling, as they are now, and a document like the Gospel of Thomas would naturally become a target of intense debate. So, it was left out of the canon precisely because it would undo what the early Church Fathers desired – a formal church, filled with adoring devotees who left the hard inner work up to the priest and Bishops and just followed instructions. But since so much effort was placed upon sustaining the organization of the church, priests and Bishops rapidly became managers of the religion, and not the deep seekers that were to instruct the masses. They became exactly what Jesus had accused the Pharisees of becoming – blind guides.

The content of the Gospel of Thomas is different, therefore, than the content of the public gospels of the New Testament. To read this Gospel one must need more intense spirituality, and not just some easy answer. One must need to push into the mystery of self in the world, for that is what this gospel is about – finding one's True Self. It is not theology in the conventional sense. It is not talk about Jesus and what his life and teachings mean, but rather his teachings themselves. It is like hearing Jesus personally and privately. It is like being taken aside and having a dialogue with this great teacher.

But with this privilege of hearing the private and personal teachings, also comes the responsibility of deciding the essential meaning for oneself – not what others think. You are not told in this Gospel that Jesus is the "Only Son of God," or that he performed countless miracles that prove his Divinity. You are left with astounding teachings, and you must decide what it all means for you. That is essentially a greater reality than to be sold a theological story that tries to prove a point and has an organizational agenda. Little wonder that even today, the Gospel of Thomas stands as the most controversial Gospel as well as the one the church least wants you to read.

To make sure that this work would be less esteemed, the authors of the canonical Gospels took aim at the author of this secret Gospel. Thomas is given the title "doubter," and said to have disbelieved the Lord's resurrection. We can see that there was deep political conflict over the nature and purpose of Christianity itself, and because Thomas (and others) were less concerned with the establishment of an organized and centralized church, his Gospel would have to be discredited by first discrediting him. This was a most effective weapon, since Thomas and the followers of this secret Christianity were unwilling to even address the issue, because to them all the physical representations of the ordinary and public gospels were merely superficial anyway. So, the orthodox church won by default. Sadly, this discrediting of Thomas remains to this day, since orthodox followers always wish to argue from the content of their public gospels, which are tainted by the political maneuvering of the early church.

But people today have become "doubters," and perhaps the "doubting" Thomas looks more like we look than the simple-minded folks who just accepted blind authority. Perhaps what began as an attempt to discredit an author through scandalizing him, now makes him look more real and essentially thoughtful. Maybe the New Testament story of Thomas' doubting will lead people to read the Gospel penned by a person they can relate to more than anyone else.

After all, it is the doubters among us who ask the questions and push deeper in the issue of truth than those who are just so willing to follow external authority, even into the abyss of ignorance and stupidity.

The Gospel of Thomas stands alone. It was originally pushed out, but now stands out. That is why it must be read. That is why it will change you, if you listen closely enough.

Insight 1

These are the hidden and private teachings that the living Jesus uttered and which Didymos Jude Thomas wrote down. And he said, "whoever finds the meaning of these sayings will not experience death."

From the Head ...

We are told that these are teachings which were written down and saved for us to read. They are not church tradition or talk about Jesus, but direct sayings of Jesus as he lived. Perhaps there was a concern even during Jesus' life that the essential message would be forgotten and mere talk of personalities would become the central concern. Thomas makes this bold statement at the very beginning so that no one will be confused as to the focus of this document. Also, Thomas is telling us that these teachings are different than the ones publicly uttered. He obviously is aware that although the public teachings are important, they are not on the same level as these, which are meant for the earnest seeker, not the casual listener or the spiritually immature.

Spirituality has as its essence the unseen, invisible and abstract reality of our being. Because it is hidden – that is, veiled from the obvious material matrix of things – it requires a kind of disciplined way of looking that is different from the everyday pattern of experiencing and interacting with the world. It is, as this insight suggests, hidden. And because it has a fundamentally different kind of reality to it than does the obvious material process, the person who begins to understand this other reality experiences a kind of conscious suspension of the ordinary world. When Jesus says "he who finds the meaning of these sayings will not experience death" he does not mean that material death will not occur, but rather that a person begins to identify themselves as beyond the domination of the physical process where death is the ruling power. In this way, one ceases to "experience death" as an event to their identity, because their identity itself has altered.

This collection of sayings or insights reveal this hidden reality and a transformed consciousness that is required to perceive the Spirit. As such, they are whispers of a reality that cannot be spoken of directly, but only pointed to. This pointing to is the intention of Jesus' private teachings, and Thomas' reason for compiling them.

From the Heart ...

After twenty years in the ministry I had reached a dead end. I could no longer believe the core of orthodox Christianity regardless of how liberal I was with the Biblical text. The basic idea that God had sent his Son to die for me seemed like just one more item to feel guilty about and even reinforced the material matrix of the death process of a hurtful and unjust world. I was falling apart, even though on the outside, publicly, I appeared serene and confident.

I had always had a sense that life itself was rather meaningless, but I was well defended from it. My head kept me aloft, and I stayed well distracted – busy. But my pain was becoming intolerable. I decided to look elsewhere. I studied everything. I learned to meditate, was initiated as a Shaman, and got a graduate degree in clinical psychology. It helped some, but something else was bugging me.

I did not realize it at the time, but that something else that was bugging me was a Spiritual presence that would change everything in my life, and dissolve my living death. Later, as I read the opening saying of the Gospel of Thomas, I understood the phrase "Whoever finds the meaning of these sayings will not experience death."

Insight 2

Jesus said, "Let him who seeks, continue seeking until he finds. When he finds, he will become troubled. When he becomes troubled, he will be astonished, and will rise above the illusion and ignorance of the world."

From the Head ...

Seeking truth and being disturbed go hand in hand. As we experience the world with all its harsh realities we become bothered by the injustice, lack of concern and utter disregard for truth and life itself. At that moment of disturbance we can either allow our hurt and frustration to push us through the ordinary layer of reality to something more, or we can become fixed into the pain and suffering. To acknowledge our human dilemma is to not only validate its hurtful reality, but also to see ourselves as witnesses to it. In seeing ourselves as caught in something and yet witnessing it from some unknown source within is truly astounding.

To simply see ourselves in the world leads to the beginning of a far deeper question: what is the "I" that sees myself in the world? In other words, the process of seeking oneself in the world leads to the revelation that there is an "I" beyond the world watching. At the very moment of recognizing this "I" beyond the world, we experience ourselves literally achieving enlightenment and reigning over every "thing." This enlightenment is a deep realization that "I" am more than all the things of the world, and in some mysterious way this "I" cannot be destroyed.

This finding and experiencing the higher "I" is both disturbing and astounding. We are not solid at one level, but a kind of pure being that has a fluidity of focus. In that realization, and only within that awakening, can true choice take place: do I wish to be the higher "I," or sink into the existence of the worldly "me?" Do I raise above the illusion and ignorance, or do I stay within the agitation and over-whelmed sense of the existing "me?" Awakening to the True Self is the most incredible experience of liberation, peace and wonderment. It is, as Jesus put it, astonishing.

From the Heart ...

Seeking truth had become my religion, but the cost was distur-bance. Everything in my life was challenged. The truth may set you free, but first it makes you angry. That was my experience. One day, out in the desert, a friend who was walking with me and just listening to my complaining, started to laugh. I asked him what was so funny, and he told me that I was. He said, "You're the funniest person I know. All wrapped up in this little self of yours – like some comedy routine." I protested, "I am not all wrapped up in myself – I don't even know what that means anymore." "Well, you're right about that," he said, "you don't know what that means at all." He stopped walking and just looked at me; a very uncomfortable staring. It was like he looked through me to something else. He told me simply: "Why don't you become interested in observing yourself? See where you are, and why you are thinking, feeling and seeing what you are. You might be surprised. Just observe. Don't do anything. Stop all this nonsense about God – so what? You're the issue, not God. Religion is for the small-minded. Drop it. It's an illusion."

I had no real sense of what he was talking about, but since I had no answers, I decided to take his advice and simply observe myself – nothing else. I became interested in what was occurring in me. Then it happened. Nothing like a great event, just a simple realization or reve-lation: there was an "I" watching the "me" go through everything. All my thoughts and feelings were just a little "me" going through some routine, exactly like my friend had said. I laughed out loud. What interested me the most was that this little "me" was so much in control of my life, and it would just worry and gyrate over everything. And all the issues – the hurt feelings and the stupid little thoughts were astounding to me. This "me" was so weird, but the larger question loomed: what was this "I" that watched? And, in what way did it exist, if it had an existence at all? What was really going on?

Insight 3

> *Jesus said, "If those who lead you say to you,*
> *'See, the kingdom is in the sky,' then the birds of the*
> *sky will precede you. If they say to you, 'It is in the sea,'*
> *then the fish will precede you. Rather, the kingdom is*
> *inside of you, and it is outside of you. When you come*
> *to know yourselves, then you will become known,*
> *and you will realize that it is you who are the*
> *children of the living light. But if you will not*
> *know yourselves, you dwell in poverty*
> *and it is you who are that poverty."*

From the Head ...

This is, in part, a familiar saying of Jesus. In the public teachings Jesus also instructed that the Kingdom was within. Privately, he emphasized this teaching with humor. The birds or the fish will get there faster than those who teach that the kingdom of God is coming on the earth in some kind of tangible and material way, he laughs. The Kingdom of Light is not a political or economic re-organization of the world, nor does it have anything to do with the physical processes of the world. It is beyond and inside and it is spread out over the world in the depth of human beings.

This inner kingdom is the dwelling place of an alien reality – alien in the true sense of that word, something that is literally not of this world. This alien is the Spirit, or spark of the divine that is part of the kingdom of Light itself. Unawakened, this spark lives in poverty – not knowing itself or its true home. It is literally lost amidst the suffering and horrible process of the tragic world, which is a kind of ignorance and depression existing outside the world of Light.

It is often referred to as "darkness" or "intoxication" in Gnostic literature.

To know the True Self is to become aware of this alien presence that transcends the psyche and the physical structure of things. It is an abstract quality of pure being that does not exist as energy or matter, and yet simply is. The poverty that is spoken of is existence in this dark world, all the matrix of matter and energy that combines to form the physical and emotional world that human beings find themselves in. To awaken is to "become known" – who you really are – a child of the kingdom of Light.

This understanding that we are Light trapped in darkness is the fundamental teaching of this entire document. We think of ourselves in ways that diminish our true being, and keep us trapped in a world that does not deserve our Light. Everything here in this world is geared to keep us asleep and lost to the truth of ourselves. Our systems of politics and economics, although designed by us as people to free us from the brutality of mere existence, only increases the hurt and suffering. There is no way out, Jesus is teaching, unless you seek inside to find something that knows itself from a world beyond this darkness of space, time and matter.

From the Heart ...

The religion that I grew up with taught that the world was a good place gone bad because of the sins of human beings. The darkness was simply human sin, and to overcome that sin God had made a dramatic historical event that would eventually change the world back into its pure goodness. Never mind that the dinosaurs were killed by some giant rock that fell out of the sky, or that evolution had eliminated millions of species. Never mind that the world process was a huge death machine long before any person walked the earth, or spotted the tragedy in a conscious kind of knowing that brought about alienation and the sin that was taught to me as a child. Somewhere I stopped buying it. Yes, the world was a kind of harmony – but a brutal one at best. Death ruled, not life – and everyone knew it, we just didn't talk about it or allow it to seep into our consciousness. Denial is the cornerstone of our darkness. Peggy Lee sang it years ago: "Is that all there is?"

I always thought of the kingdom within as just an attitude or decision toward life. That's a good liberal interpretation, but a positive attitude can be just as diseased as a negative attitude, particularly when it involves avoidance of truth. My having discovered a higher "I" within was just the beginning of a journey into another reality.

I remember asking people: "Do you sometimes feel that you don't belong here?" I thought it was a weird question, but most people didn't think so – they almost always said, "Yeah, often." Feeling like you don't belong or don't fit in is a rather simple way of saying alien-ation. We feel alienated. For the most part alienation is seen as a psychological disorder, or problem that can be solved through becoming "well adjusted" or having a different environment of friends or family. But alienation is not a negative word, as I discov-ered. Instead of it being something wrong with me, I found that it was what was right with me. That which sensed alienation was truly alien, and that was a revelation that began to lift my spiritual poverty. The kingdom of Light was literally inside of me!

Insight 4

*Jesus said, "The man old in age will not hesitate
to ask a small child seven days old about the place of life,
and he will live. For many who are first will become
last, and they will become one and the same."*

From the Head ...

Reality is a learned concept that we create and sustain through social agreement. Social consensual reality is a strong force of perception. It literally tells us what and how to think. When this insight suggests that an old man will not hesitate to ask a child about life, it points to the truth that we become exhausted with the hardness of our perceptions and our forgetfulness about the source of who we really are. We live in a world of illusional meanings and contrived importance. Very small children who are not trained in this social consensual reality have a kind of loose flowing to them, which simply means that they have not hardened yet. They have not development an ego or small self to which to align themselves with the social world. Images are more fluid and dynamic. They see what we have trained ourselves not to see.

Someone who is strong in the social consensual world is usually the last one to let go their reality set. They have derived power in their focus, and have learned to manipulate that contrived reality to keep it alive and growing. Literally, they will be the last to see. And yet, they, too, will become one and the same with the larger scope of spiritual presence even if they are last.

In his public teachings Jesus said: "Blessed are the poor in spirit." Those who are weak in this social consensual reality have a greater chance of seeing something beyond the "hardness" more quickly because they need to – they have little power in the contrived world of things. That is a blessing if we let it be. Alcoholics, drug addicts and those who have lost their way are literally closer to the truth than those who have success and popular appeal. Awakening to the vastness of our True Self saves us from the suffering that's caused by the ignorant force of this world. How? By simply allowing ourselves to let go of its meaning. The world and all its contrived social agreements mean absolutely nothing. They have power because we give them power.

From the Heart ...

I found that my troubled seeking of the truth and my "falling apart" was the greatest aid to my Spirit. When I no longer knew what to think and feel I was freed to simply be. At first, of course, it terrorized me. I had always been told what was what. I didn't realize that I wasn't free at all. I was a slave to the ignorance of the world, and all my education and power in the world were just more evidence of that enslavement. That which I thought was my strength was really my weakness. I came to realize what that saying meant: the first shall be last and the last shall be first. I was smart and articulate and those things were my greatest enemies even as I needed them to aid me along my way. A strange kind of conundrum.

When my son was born I began to experience his lack of agreed upon reality, and how everything was geared to teach him what we had all consented to. He was free in ways that I could not imagine, and I found myself being angry at him when he "disobeyed." Everything about our child rearing is an attempt to get our children to obey our rules and regulations – all contrived of course. Some children obey them in a negative way through "acting out," but most obey them by becoming good little drones for the system. It is a kind of power trap that only spiritual enlightenment can save you from. You cannot be a rebel within the system. You have to step out to be a real rebel.

I use to laugh at someone who asked me "are you saved?" They meant, of course, whether I believed in their religious construct. Now

I see that question in a different light: am I saved from the ignorance of not seeing the contrivance of the world? The question now has relevance to me. I am an old man asking a small child about life. That saves me.

Insight 5

Jesus said, "Recognize what is in your sight, and that which is hidden from you will become plain to you. For there is nothing hidden which will not become manifest."

From the Head ...

The conflicts we have on the outside of us are the conflicts that we have on the inside of us. Our social consensual world is a world of inside-out living, whether we realize it or not. This insight asks us to simply look at our lives – see what is in plain sight and ask ourselves about its place of origin. We manifest our social world through projecting a hidden agreement underneath.

We agree to our place within the social reality. Abused people agree, on some level, to their abuse. Powerful people agree to their power. That is not to place blame. It is simply an observation of how the world works its dark magic on us. We get convinced that we have to agree, or die. Sometimes that is physically true, sometimes just metaphorically true. Oddly, the disillusion and ignorance of the world creates a kind of inability of sight. We just don't see. Our agreement creates not only hardened facts in our lives, but also abstract ideas that manifest themselves in relationships, jobs and self concepts. Nothing we have inside stays inside. Our abstract ideas and thoughts become projected realities.

From the Heart ...

After walking away from my contrived life, with all its agreements and "contracts," I began to see just how much that stuff was hidden in me. The failed relationships were agreed upon long before the relationships began. I picked people designed to fulfill the contract, and they picked me, too.

It became important to me just to look at my life – nothing fancy; just see what I had agreed to. It horrified me. How could I let myself get into that? What was I thinking? Well, I was on auto-pilot guided by the hidden force of the agreed-upon social contract. I was playing my role(s).

As a therapist I worked with many people who were caught in abusive relationships and just simply felt impotent to get out. At first I thought it was a courage issue, but of course it was much more severe than that. Literally caught in a web of social/political and economic agreement, people cannot break free without first breaking the inner bonds that hold them. It is not that people lack courage. In fact, I have found that people generally have remarkable courage when they finally see, and I mean really see, what holds them in slavery. But to come to that sight is the greatest difficulty that we face.

What makes us want to see, or need to see? I guess that's an individual answer. For some it takes a great deal, for others not as much. For me, well, it took a lot. Like most, I was particularly caught in something I could not see, and therefore would not believe that it was real at all.

Insight 6

His disciples questioned him and asked, "Do you want us to fast? How shall we give alms? What diet shall we observe?" Jesus said, "Do not do what you hate, and don't lie to yourself. For all things are plain in the sight of your true being. Remember, nothing hidden will not become manifest, and nothing covered will remain without being uncovered."

From the Head ...

We externalize our spirituality through making it religious. We set about making rules and religious doctrine, which just becomes a part of the social consensual reality instead of freeing us. Jesus' disciples were desiring external things to do that would validate their egos, but Jesus turned it toward them by telling them to seek their own knowledge of what was truly hateful to their spiritual truth. "Don't lie to yourself" and "Don't do what you hate," these are things that each individual must do for themselves.

The spiritual truth that Jesus taught was very personal, in that it requires each person to assume responsibility for knowing their inner life. It's hard work to ask the questions: am I lying to myself about my life? Am I doing what is spiritually authentic, or am I involved with doing something hateful to that Spirit?

The primacy of self knowledge over external morality and behavioral social correctness is a cornerstone of Jesus' insight here. Much like Insight 3 wherein Jesus asserts that not knowing yourself makes you dwell in poverty, this insight rubs hard at our inauthentic natures. We become what we hate, which is an old rabbinical saying. So, it is best to not lie to yourself, and not become the hatred that we can place upon ourselves. Again, nothing hidden will not become manifest.

From the Heart ...

Even as a religious liberal, I had routinized my spirituality. Everything was a formula. I didn't realize that, of course, but it was true. I was lying to myself all the time, and I most certainly practiced a life that offended my Spirit. I was not free at all, even though I would have argued with anyone who said that I wasn't.

Strange how this happens to us. How subtle is the system of agreements that we make in the world. How easy it is to live an inauthentic life, and play as if our lives are real and truthful. But I'm a good person! Goodness matters not one bit. Nor does all the social talk of being an adjusted good citizen. Thoreau said in his writings at Walden Pond that if he was to repent of anything it would be of his good behavior. He wondered: "What demon possessed me that I behaved so well?" He was seeing what Jesus meant in this insight. We're a bunch of phonies playing as if we know when we don't have a clue. It is not until we break out of the systemic spiritual mockery that our True Self can help us become changed into an authentic being.

The hardest thing for me was to admit that I was playing at religion and spirituality. It was just a ploy to get me power or massage my ego. I ended up justifying things that I hated. I played at politics inside and outside the church institution without being aware that I was doing so. How inauthentic is that? What demon, indeed, possessed me that I agreed to all this so easily?

21

Insight 7

> *Jesus said, "Blessed is the lion which becomes man when consumed by man; and cursed is the man whom the lion consumes, and the lion becomes man."*

From the Head ...

The lion is a symbol of courage and strength. To defeat a lion requires a great act of bravery, or to have the heart of a lion is to be a person of conviction and courage. But this insight goes beyond that symbolism.

The dark ignorance of the world is symbolically represented as a lion here. It is fierce and monstrous. It will consume you if it can. Cursed is the person who lets the world consume him, and blessed is the person who can live in this world and walk through it awakened to her higher self. It is a struggle to come to the truth. To defeat the ignorance of the world is like consuming a lion – beating it in battle. For Jesus, there is a kind of esoteric spiritual warfare occurring in which each of us is individually and collective involved. St. Paul wrote that it was not against flesh and bone that we struggle, but against powers and principalities.

To overcome the world requires not only courage, but self-knowledge. Courage without this knowledge is just a battle, making that which is resisted the definitive scope of the struggle. But for Jesus and the spiritually enlightened the struggle is always symbolically played out in everything we do, think and feel. Truly, we struggle against powers and unseen forces. Even our own false psychological selves take on a personality of their own. Our fight is always personal, and if the lion consumes us, we are cursed by our own inauthentic existence, and the dissolution of self knowledge that is the result of that consumption.

From the Heart ...

Most of my life, whether I realized it or not, was ruled by guilt, shame and automatic responses. It consumed me and I was, indeed, cursed because of it. I stayed in relationships that I should have never entered into. I said and did things that were meant to please and smooth over conflict, but were just as inauthentic as could be.

It is said in pop-psychological circles that people "stuff" their feelings. That may be true, but it is not the essential problem. The real problem lies in the fact that it is people who are being stuffed into the mouth of the ignorance of the world, and literally eaten down to their heels. The feelings that most people are said to "stuff" simply makes them more juicy for the lion to eat. The world loves fat and juicy stuffed people who, like myself, couldn't see that they were being lined up to be a hot lunch for the world beast of social consensual reality. Like fatted cattle being led to the slaughter, our awareness is consumed and digested by the world. I was just going along minding my own business, I thought; but who was I really minding?

It is not until we realize that we have to battle for our freedom and for self-knowledge that we can enter into the arena where the victory can be won. Until then, we are cursed by being consumed. Controlled, robotic and mindless – these are all attributes of having been consumed by the lion. "Eat donuts and be happy," as one friend put it. That curse gets us spiritually slaughtered and cut up into small parts to be eaten. If you have ever felt that you were torn apart, you probably were. If you have ever felt that you were being sucked dry, you probably were. Blessed is the person who awakens to the lion's attack, and himself becomes the courage and strength of that lion. Each of us has to come to terms with what it means to acquire the lion's courage. What act of bravery will I need to make? What movement of my Spirit is needed to save myself from being consumed? It is a dramatic scene that each of us plays out. We are either eaten or not: that is the simple truth. There is no middle ground.

Insight 8

> *And he said, "The man is a wise fisherman
> who cast his net into the sea and drew it up from the
> sea full of small fish. Among them the wise fisherman
> found a fine large fish. He threw all the small fish back
> into the sea and chose the large fish without difficulty.
> Whoever has ears to hear, let him hear."*

From the Head ...

There are many things happening in each of our lives. Not all are of equal value, nor does each and every issue deserve our attention and focus. Which issues matter, and which ones don't – that is the subject of this insight.

There is an old saying, "don't sweat the small stuff." With an addendum that reads: "most stuff is small stuff." This is what this insight is driving at. We tend to, as Jesus in his public teachings scoffed, strain at a gnat to swallow a camel. That is how we are in dealing with our lives. All the issues of how and where and when are not really important. It is the larger questions of why that we avoid. Given the opportunity, which we all have, we choose to throw the big fish back and keep all the small ones. So, our lives become petty and small. Kierkegaard wrote that we "tranquilize ourselves with the trivial," and that we become "shut-up" and filled with the sickness that is unto death which is despair. It is a wise person, indeed, who can ascertain which issue is deserving and needs to have attention, and which ones should be just thrown back into the sea.

Again, Jesus asks us to listen. He is saying that to be wise is not difficult – it is a choice. It requires our mindfulness and our attention.

We have to let go of those things that drive us toward the social consensual world and really look for ourselves. When we do, he says, we can become wise, and throw back the smallness of our reality, and come to terms with the larger reality of the Spirit.

Each of us, then, is a fisherman. Are we wise, or foolish and ignorant of what will truly satisfy our hunger? Are we listening?

From the Heart ...

Its hard to listen, and it's hard to know the difference between a big fish and small fish when it comes to looking at ourselves. The real issues are rarely the ones we think they are. We worry about things that don't matter, and just avoid the things that do. I've been that way in my life. I didn't know it, but it was the small things that drove me. Like what? Job, security, money, love – yes, love. I thought I knew what was important in those terms, but I didn't. Love, for me, was not at all an issue of spirituality. Not really. I have to be honest about this. If it were I wouldn't have been so miserable in all my relationships. Love was more about comfort, support, sex, romance and ego. I hate to write that, but it's true, and I think it's true for most of us if we're honest.

For me to keep the big fish required an act of truly throwing everything else away so the water could get clear, and I could see and hear again. I had to leave those things that I had defined my life around, and seek a new definition. I'm not saying everyone will have to do that – of course not. But each person will have to decide what keeping the big fish and throwing the rest back into the sea, means in their life. That can be hard, because we can convince ourselves that having a lot of little fishes is better than that one big fish – but it isn't and can't be. The one big fish is always our True Self. Everything else is the small fry.

Insight 9

Jesus said, "Now a sower went out, took a handful of seeds, and scattered them. Some fell on the road; the birds came and gathered them up. Others fell on rock, did not take root in the soil, and did not produce ears. And others fell on thorns; they choked the seeds and worms ate them. And others fell on good soil and it produced good fruit: it bore a great abundance.

From the Head ...

This teaching, like all of Jesus' teachings, has an internal and external meaning. On the surface we think of a person spreading a message. Some people listen, others don't. This insight suggests that image. However, it has a deeper meaning as well, particularly when we remember that this is a teaching to his closest disciples and friends. He is asking them to see what bears fruit inside of them.

We need to ask, perhaps, what is the seed that is being scattered? On this count, the seed is not just a message but a spiritual reality. We see that we have scattered our true selves everywhere. Some of our spiritual reality lies on the many roads we have traveled – lost to us as if eaten by worms or birds, or just dried up. The point being, be careful who you share your energy with, for in the sharing of it, you also scatter it, and cannot be retrieved again without great intentionality and effort.

Also this insight suggests how dangerous the world is to the Spirit. The fact that spiritual truth has been devoured and lost, should cause us to take pause and reflect. To see the tragedy of the world is to see that it has consumed the truth – like seed eaten by worms.

For people who want spirituality to be a soft, warm and fuzzy feeling, Jesus has a clear and harsh wake-up call. You are the seed scattered. Where are you? Are you being eaten by the world worm, or wakening to bear fruit? It is a tough question that is being asked in this insight, but an important one.

From the Heart . . .

Most of us are eaten down to our heels. That's a strange image – just a bunch of heels walking around, our awareness consumed and all but digested by the world system. I was nearly gone at one point, I think. I thought I was so real and authentic, but I was just a pair of heels walking around. You know that you are heels walking around impersonating a real person when you're tired all the time. When you have a schedule that doesn't give you time to reflect and controls your life – you're heels. Robotic, mechanical, not alive. That is being eaten down to your heels. More: you have no sense of what is really happening other than the ordinary worries of the world. The ancient Gnostics called it "forgetfulness" or "intoxication."

Depression is the major symptom of being intoxicated by the world. I was depressed, angry and tired. But I put on a happy face – you know, that smiling little yellow dot with no real substance and no body, just a smiling face with big black lifeless eyes. All smile. Heels.

Don Juan taught Carlos Castaneda that a gesture to the Spirit was always a necessary precondition of real movement. He was right. That gesture is to throw back all the little fish and concentrate on the big fish – the Spirit itself. After all, what do you have to lose? Just your heels. For me, that gesture was to get out of everything I was doing. To stop my world, and retreat so I could heal and get a different vision. People were angry, upset and puzzled by my actions. Mid-life crisis was there observation. I didn't care. It was more than some mid-life crisis, but I didn't need to argue or explain. Gestures to the Spirit require movement, not explanations.

Most people live their whole lives not really knowing who they are. They take their depression as something that needs to be medicated, or solved. But depression is the first step, like alienation, into the answer. To follow the depression, and use it. Make it point the way. That is a scary thing to most folks. But, it is a necessary precondition. A gesture to the Spirit.

Insight 10

> *Jesus said, "I have cast fire upon the world,*
> *and see, I am guarding it until it blazes."*

From the Head ...

Fire is often a metaphor for the Spirit, or spiritual work. Fire burns you. It heats you up. It transforms things from hardened wood into burning coals, smoke and light, and produces heat. In this teaching to his friends, Jesus is saying something they already know – that their world is coming to an end. He has brought them to themselves, and now that True Self is burning their small, social consensual world up into smoke.

Acknowledging the Spirit changes us. You cannot acknowledge the Spirit and remain unchanged. If you have, then you never saw anything at all. But this insight also suggests that the burning Spirit must be tended and guarded. Left in the world it can go back to sleep, become forgetful again. But once going, it also spreads to that which is nearby. The Spirit blazes.

From the Heart ...

It took years of tending before my Spirit blazed. More smoke than fire, for the most part. To see with spiritual eyes is to feel the blaze. Not to look at the world with ordinary eyes of concern for security, and all the things that we are taught to see: this is to watch the Spirit blaze.

Guarding the fire is doing all the work necessary to keep it going. I observed that most things were meant to keep me from seeing and tending to that fire. Ordinary things that are called good and valuable, work, family and social responsibility can all be aspects of the ordinary reality that is the enemy of the fire. I am not saying that those things are bad in and of themselves, but when they become consuming and the focus of life, then the fire goes out. It's as simple as that.

Emerson wrote: To thine own self be true. That is guarding the fire until it blazes. Being true to the True Self – to the non-ordinary reality – is our only real job. To get clear on that was difficult for me. It seemed so selfish, but in reality it was not selfish at all – self giving is closer to the truth. How interesting it is that we are guarded from knowing our True Self, from a social consensual reality and world system that needs the use of that spiritual reality, but needs it to remain unawakened for control and usage. When I stopped feeding the consensual reality in my life as it was, I was shocked to see how fast it started to die. It cannot live without the Spirit, nor can it survive with the Spirit awake. When the Spirit begins to awaken, it needs to be guarded, or back to sleep it will go. Guard your Spirit! That is Jesus' advice – I take it literally.

Insight 11

Jesus said, "This heaven will pass away, and the one above it will pass away. The dead are not alive, and the living will not die. In the days when you consumed what is dead, you made it what is alive. When you come to dwell in the light, what will you do? On the day when you were one you became two. But when you become two, what will you do?"

From the Head . . .

All of our contrived realities will pass away, as well as the physical matrix of the universe. Our "heaven" – the consensual reality of our social order, our laws and economic structures, are just defense mechanisms. They will dissolve with the awakening of the Spirit. But more than this: the dark reality of the world was never alive to begin with. It derived its life from the Spirit, and when the Spirit withdraws from it, it dies.

Jesus says in this insight that "in the days when you consumed what (was) dead, you made it alive," meaning that life apart from the Spirit has no essential life at all. Like depression which cannot exist apart from the larger psyche, as if it were a separate entity, the world cannot exist apart from the Spirit that is trapped in its darkness.

Another part of this insight deals with the fact that we are scattered within ourselves, and are split off from the wholeness that is the essential reality of our True Self. The longing we have for the opposite sex and for others is not only a darkness of the biological nature of things that propels people into sexual intrigue, possessiveness and even violence for the sake of survival, but it also splits us within ourselves. The image of Eve being ripped from Adam's body is a powerful influence here. Eve represents the Spirit and Adam the soul. The soul is literally lost without the Spirit that can give it true life. As the Spirit awakens to the light, free awareness begins. Until then authenticity is asleep and withered, and everything about us is controlled and enslaved. Jesus is asking an important question to reflect upon – what will you do when your freedom is restored, and the split is repaired by the light? It's a good question.

From the Heart ...

As I reflect upon the impact of this insight in my life, I realize how much difficulty I have had with the split of the masculine and feminine principles within me. Carl Jung, the Swiss psychotherapist, spoke of this as the Anima/Animus. My seeking to touch that anima within, that spiritual quality that feels transcendent of my soul stuff and is a feminine essence, was always being projected out into my falling in love, and my subsequent disappointments. Relationships failed because they could not connect me to what was truly the issue – my spiritual detachment. I remember dreaming of a dark woman who filled me with sexual excitement, but who disappeared mysteriously into unknown quarters as I was left helplessly wanting her. Repeatedly in my dream material I was trying to bring this figure into the light. A friend asked me, "And if you get her – what happens?" That was, of course, Jesus' question to his friends – what will you do? The answer is just now unfolding in my life. What happens? Well, everything changes, but to what I am not sure. I suppose each of us has to answer that question for ourself. Everything else, as this insight suggests, just passes away.

Insight 12

The disciples said to Jesus, "We know that you will depart from us. Who is to be our leader?" Jesus said to them, "Wherever you are, you are to go to James the righteous, for whose sake heaven and earth came into being."

From the Head ...

Who is James the righteous, and why is he important? Not much is known about this figure in reality; however it may well be that the James that Jesus is referring to is the Essene Teacher of Righteousness. James is a figure symbolic of spiritual enlightenment representing a continuation of Jesus' teachings and his work as awakener/redeemer.

Of interest is the question itself in that it suggests our need of teachers and guides. While it is true that all of these teachings in this personal Gospel are meant to lead people to their own inner spark, it is relevant to understand that along our way we have need of others who can help us. But not all teachers are enlightened. There are many false guides who lead people into their control and manipulation rather than to true inner knowledge. Obviously for Jesus, James the righteous represents an authentic being from the world of light beyond the darkness, and that is why he would say that heaven and earth are realities beneath him, which is indicated by the reference "for whose sake heaven and earth came into being."

From the Heart ...

I had many great teachers along the way. Some never thought of themselves as teachers at all, but were nevertheless very good instructors in the ways of the Spirit. There are many who claim to have gnosis – acquaintance with the Spirit, but the truth is, authentic teachers of spiritual wisdom are few and far between. Most are just people who have some skill or talent that they take to be spiritual, but which has very little to do with authentic spiritual knowledge. Many people confuse soul knowledge with spiritual knowledge, and there is a profound difference. Soul knowledge, while important and instrumental in our journey in this world, is a creation and function of this reality. It is an energy force or psychic wrap that is the link to the Spirit, but not the Spirit itself – which is, as I have said, an alien reality beyond any description within the categories of matter and energy.

Who taught me about the Spirit? I can't answer that question. I take it to be a very private matter, and for the most part, I was led into inner revelations not by human individuals, but by a presence that defies my ability to define it. Perhaps that is how it works. I know that there have been times when I longed to have someone to go to for some authentic knowledge, and from time to time that happened. But it was rare.

Insight 13

*Jesus said to his disciples, "Compare me to someone
and tell me whom I am like." Simon Peter said to him,
"You are like a righteous angel." Matthew said to him,
"You are like a wise philosopher." Thomas said to him,
"Master, my mouth is wholly incapable of saying
whom you are like." Jesus said, "I am not your master.
Because you have drunk, you have become intoxicated
from the bubbling spring which I have measured out."
And he took him and withdrew and told him three things.
When Thomas returned to his companions, they asked him,
"What did Jesus say to you?" Thomas said to them,
"If I tell you one of the things which he told me, you
will pick up stones and throw them at me; a fire
will come out of the stones and burn you up."*

From the Head . . .

This insight is different from the public Gospel presentation of the
same story. In the public Gospel story, Peter is said to have been
blessed by recognizing that Jesus is "The Christ," whereas the others
are left behind in a quandary. This insight has Thomas as the person
who recognizes something important about Jesus, but cannot find
language to express it, meaning that ordinary words are inadequate
to describe spiritual realities. Jesus then recognizes Thomas as a true
companion, and no longer a student and follower.

The political nature of the public Gospels is very evident in this
conflicting text. Peter, in the canon, represents an externalized
religion where it is said that a church will be built upon him. In this
Gospel, Jesus is not concerned about building a church at all, but

moving beyond the master role into a co-journeying with those who drink from his mouth and become like him.

Thomas and Jesus talk privately. The text reveals little about their talk, except that if the others were to learn what Jesus told Thomas, they would be angry and possibly even violent. In turn, Thomas says, their own issues, represented by the stones, would burn them up.

From the Heart ...

Along the way I discovered, as many others have, that church is not the point of spirituality, nor is religion. As a minister, most of my time was spent reinforcing the need for church. To be sure, some enlightenment went on, but it was in spite of church, and not because of it. I say that because so much of church is merely about sustaining the institution itself, and is not about an authentic gathering of people seeking the inner wisdom of the Spirit. I am not bitter about this or angry; this is just an observation. Most spiritual work is done in a solitary fashion, away from the demands of social, political and economic contrivances. Church and the religion it represents are just a function of the social consensual reality that is part of the darkness. I wish this were not true, but it is.

Owning property, paying ministers and even the collective doing of good works, are all part of playing the game and sustaining the dark system. People have thrown stones at me, metaphorically speaking, for having said this. But it is, nevertheless, true.

Nothing in this world is substantially meaningful. I know that shocks. All our systems, religious and otherwise, have nothing to do with spiritual truth. Every great spiritual teacher has taught that, and yet it is ignored and then turned around, like it was with the early Christian movement, to be made into a function of the darkness itself. But that is what darkness does. It takes light and eats it and, by eating it, hides it from view. The church is a way darkness ate Jesus' truth. I finally got that.

Insight 14

> Jesus said to them, "If you fast, you will give
> rise to sin for yourselves; and if you pray, you will be
> condemned; and if you give alms, you will do harm
> to your Spirit. When you go into any land and walk
> in the districts, if they receive you, eat what they
> will set before you, and heal the sick among them.
> For what goes into your mouth will not defile
> you, but that which issues from your mouth –
> it is that which will defile you."

From the Head ...

All of our religions give rise to self-condemnation. Our efforts to connect us to the divine often do more to separate us. The essence of this insight is that our external efforts at spirituality are pointless, because authentic spirituality is about knowing one's True Self. Whether we fast, pray or give generously to the poor – so what? That has nothing to do with the Spirit. For some that will be a strange insight, because we are taught that spirituality has to do with being a good person, or being morally upright. Those are all secondary and incidental. Spirituality has to do with who you are as a being, not what you do. While it is true that doing good and generous things are worthy attributes, in and of themselves they are not the point of understanding one's true nature.

The last part of this insight is similar with public teachings. Its not what you eat that defiles you, but what you say of yourself and what you know of yourself that defiles you. Jewish tradition and law were riddled with rules about eating. Jesus' having taught to eat what is put in front of you is in direct conflict with religious rules on such matters.

But as is often the case, authentic spirituality conflicts with the political, social, economic and religious order of the world system.

From the Heart ...

The essence of spirituality is the knowing of who you are, and where you find yourself, and where you are going. Everything else is just stuff. All the errors we commit, and the bad stuff we do, requires forgiveness for only one purpose, so that we will let go of it. Forgiveness is an unnecessary item for the Spirit, but it is important for our psychic/soul since it helps us to let go of this world system, and see our Spirit beyond all this stuff.

Guilt, shame and self-hatred are all part of the system that keeps the Spirit locked away from knowing itself. That Christianity became a religion of self-recrimination and self-condemnation speaks clearly that it has very little to do with the teachings and insights of Jesus.

I had to look at all the self-hatred and self-sabotage that was at the core of my thinking, feeling and imagining of myself. How locked into patterns I had become. I, who talked repeatedly about freedom, was not free at all. To suggest, as religions often do, that our will is free is ignorance. We are not so free as we claim. Freedom is won at the cost of dying to this world – which is what Jesus and every other great teacher has taught. There is nothing you can do to manipulate the world to let you be free. Money, power, sex, big homes and great jobs mean nothing when it comes to the issue of freedom. The only real issue is letting go of the world, and knowing yourself as truly alien from all its processes and demands. That was a hard concept for me to come to, but it was a gift of the Spirit itself.

Insight 15

> Jesus said, "When you see one who was
> not born of women, prostrate yourselves
> on your faces and worship him.
> That one is your father."

From the Head ...

Birth in the world is an act of creation. Jesus in this insight is making an important distinction between spiritual reality and physical form. The Spirit never "becomes" flesh as the public Gospels theologize. To see the Spirit one has to look past all physical reality into a separate reality that is alien to the processes of the material world. Jesus is saying, until you see this spiritual truth, you have not seen. Every material form is mere shadow.

In later Gnostic thinking on the subject, the earthly Jesus was said to host a spiritual reality we call The Christ – a presence of something beyond all creation and existence as is understood by material and energy processes. Because of this, Gnostics were falsely accused of saying that Jesus himself was unsubstantial and just an apparition. That is a misunderstanding of the point, and a political maneuver to make Gnostic thinking seem oddball and weird. The truth of the Gnostic point on this matter, and Jesus' point here in this insight, is that spiritual reality is beyond physical representations of it. The Father and Mother of Light are beyond all forms and shadows, and to worship the form is to miss the real presence, as orthodox Christianity has repeatedly done throughout the ages. That is why creeds, doctrines and dogmas are all mere shadow expressions and cannot be taken as true spirituality.

From the Heart ...

Most of us wouldn't admit that we are superficial and shallow. Appearance is important, and we worship form more than we know. Our tendency is to make our ideas of God our God, and to fashion a form around them we call religion. In point of spiritual truth, this is a great darkness that has wrapped itself around humankind from the beginning.

Without my knowing it consciously, I was worshipping all the religious ideas I said bothered me so much. I say that because it had me. In a way, it owned me. It took me 25 years to walk away from it. I am surprised at how long it took me to quit worshipping false gods, and really see the unseen, unborn, uncreated Spirit. I was always looking for an event or experience in ways that seemed compatible with my sensibility. Oddly, of course, that is just ego projection, if you will – created form. I discovered that anything solid was really a shadow when it came to the Spirit, and that which seemed like a shadow was actually more substantial. I started paying attention to things that were somehow between the lines, instead of the obvious. As Carl Jung once said, we often confuse the finger pointing at the moon, with the moon. That is what Jesus was getting at in this insight. It took me a long time to get it.

Insight 16

*Jesus said, "Men think, perhaps, that it is peace
which I have come to cast upon the world. They do
not know that it is dissension which I have come to cast
upon the earth: fire, sword, and war. For there will be five
in a house: three will be against two, and two against
three, the father against the son, and the son against
the father. And they will stand solitary."*

From the Head ...

Truth defines the falsehood. It draws a distinction, a line between
the two. Spiritual truth disrupts the systemic flow of the world order
by challenging its basic principles, namely that it is primary reality.
People who practice their spirituality are often blamed for causing
trouble by not abiding by the normal range of behaviors and actions
in the world. After all, if you take the public Gospel's story of Jesus'
life as any indication of this "dissension," you can see that the disruption began long before his ministry started. Imagine just leaving your
family, quitting your job, and wandering off into the wilderness being
called by some unseen force. Even in the Gospel of Mark it says that
his family sent agents to seize him thinking that he was crazy. Jesus
had become a troublemaker for his family. He wasn't playing his part,
which was being a good little robot for the system.

It's rather odd, I think, that Jesus is used as a symbol of "family
values" and traditional living, when in fact, taken from the orthodox
stories themselves, Jesus was anything but a normal behaving
person. He is excused from his behavior by orthodox folks because he
is seen as having a special mission to be the savior of the world. But
for the authentically spiritual, each person has claim to this same defi-

nition – a Christ. So disruption among families, political and social structures, and economic systems is to be expected.

The last sentence of this insight reveals the foreboding nature of the Spirit's demand. To seek the Spirit and the truth of self, is to stand outside of all convention and ordinary reality. It is to "stand solitary." Spirituality does not feel good. It forces you to confront the darkness, and with the darkness exposed, it attacks and blames. Conformity is the greatest weapon of the lie. To break conformity is to be a disruption and a malcontent. All conformity to the world pattern is sleep and intoxication.

Jesus says that the Spirit in him does not bring peace or unity, but separation and conflict. The conflict is of a spiritual nature, not what the world has seen through religious wars, crusades and inquisitions. Those are just world patterns reinforced by religious action. The conflict Jesus asserts is caused by disconnection and non-attachment. He will teach this principle many times in the course of this private wisdom.

From the Heart ...

When I started talking about leaving my church obligations, and by then having lead many down the path of Gnostic truth, some people were angry and accusative. I, of course, was not abandoning them at all, but just giving them a gift of practicing the knowledge I had taught. People don't like it when you walk away from things they take to be your responsibility. To be sure, this is not license to practice hurtful things, or to leave devastation everywhere. Actually, the principle of non-attachment that Jesus is suggesting here is simply one of touching the world as lightly as possible. But there are a lot of psychic vampires out there who feed on people's energy, and keep them trapped into social bondage through guilt, shame, threats and anger.

Until I walked away from my old life, I couldn't see how draining and intoxicated I had become with all the emotional and intellectual demands. For some I was "falling apart," but I knew the truth – I was coming together. It just wasn't pleasing to those who were surrounding me like a crowd of hungry vultures feeding on my last drops of blood. I found that mock spirituality builds big churches and becomes politically powerful. True spirituality puts you at odds with just about everything. That is what Jesus was getting at in this insight. He is right.

Insight 17

*Jesus said, "I shall give you what
no eye has seen and what no ear has heard
and what no hand has touched and what has
never occurred to the human mind."*

From the Head ...

This saying is also referenced in the public Gospels, but it is made to seem far more fleshly and material there than it was meant to be. This insight refers to the truth that spiritual reality cannot be found – whether through philosophical reflection or endeavors of desiring devotees. The spiritual reality that Jesus refers to presents itself through revelatory experience. The best one can do is simply wait upon it in openness and acceptance.

When we talk of walking a spiritual path, generally speaking it means that one is walking a path of openness to the Spirit; of listening and being aware of the non-ordinary nature of the Spirit itself. Many today, as in ancient times, seek to teach people that it is spiritual to see wonder and awe in simple creative things; to feel intensely the marvels of nature and the complexities of life. All that is soul stuff, not authentic spirituality – for the Spirit is not nature's process, except in a dark kind of fashion.

There is so much confusion on this subject, which is all part of the world system's defense against self knowledge, and a trap of the darkness. To experience the wonders of nature says nothing of the Spirit, which is far more wondrous than anything presented in all the material and energy processes of the universe. Every place of great energy is not to be thought of as a spiritual reality in and of itself, but merely a portal through which the Spirit might be seen. In actual fact, places of great energy that seem to be very spiritual are places where the fabric of the universe is weakest. That is why we are drawn to them – like the desert experience of the mystics. Our thinking plays tricks on us, since we cannot understand what is happening with our human mind; we simply conceive of the experience as being somehow connected to the place or to nature – when that is not the point at all.

Jesus is attempting to be as clear as possible about this truth. He is saying that the Spirit reveals itself in ways not known to the human mind, and so must be understood with another kind of mind – a spiritual mind that is asleep until awakened. As is said in various texts on this matter, the Spirit knocks or calls in an attempt to awaken the Spirit within. Not until this call is heard by the inner Spirit can anything truly be seen. For the Spirit knows itself and its world, and the world knows itself and its reality, and there is a line between the two that can only be breached by the fullness of the Spirit. This is the function of the redeemer figure in spiritual thinking – to cross the limit and reveal authentic knowledge of the world of Light.

From the Heart ...

Many of my teachers laughed at me. They thought I was funny, particularly as I tried to figure things out on some rational level. My greatest enemy was my intellect and my academic way of thinking. I was trained all too well. A puppet of the world way of thinking. It's funny how in this awakening process for me, I went from thinking that I knew truth, to being so utterly confused, to simply letting go of the whole idea of trying to make sense out of it, to finally having it just appear from someplace within me as a revealed knowing.

I feel as though I have lived this insight, and seen it played out in my life for the last few years. What I see I have not found – it found me. What I know, I did not come to – it came to me. What I have heard, I did not strain to hear – it shouted in my face. Truly, the Spirit is a separate reality beyond the scope of our human mind, and does not exist the way we reckon existence to be by any measure of observation or ordinary experience. As Thomas said when trying to describe what his experience of The Christ was like, my mouth is totally incapable of saying what this spiritual world is like. It is, that is all I can say of it.

Insight 18

The disciples said to Jesus, "Tell us how our end will be."
Jesus said, "Have you discovered, then, the beginning,
that you look for the end? For where the beginning is,
there will the end be. Blessed is he who will take
his place in the beginning; he will know the
end and will not experience death."

From the Head ...

It is not the end that tells us who we are, it is our origin. End-time talk, which is so fashionable among the ordinary dominant religions of the western world, does not help with the deepest questions of our beingness. It only plays into our fear. When we see the truth of our near obsession with end-time thinking, we see that behind it all is a kind of homesickness for a different kind of reality; a reality that is radically different than the current world in which we find ourselves – an original reality beyond our present dilemma. It is this original beginning, where death and suffering are not part of the functional structure, that Jesus is talking about.

Knowing where you come from and who you really are makes a greater difference in terms of our current journey, than knowing when our journey here will end. For without knowing who you are and where you come from, life is merely suffering and hopeless. To know, as Jesus is suggesting, that you are essentially Spirit and not subject to the laws of this world's system is a remarkable knowledge – a liberating truth. Indeed, it takes the bite out of the pain and confusion of this world, and allows one to experience the pure joy of being, as Valentinus put it in his Gospel of Truth: "that perfect day."

To take your place in the beginning, which Jesus says is blessed, is simply to move your knowledge into the deeper part of yourself – into the Spirit. That is the truth of you, your True Self – the spark of the divine. It cannot die nor be used up or consumed – it just is. When you know that essential truth, all talk of when the world will end becomes unimportant, because in a manner of speaking it has already ended with your recognition that you do not belong to it. Truly, that is a great blessing!

From the Heart ...

When I was little I had a red sweater that buttoned up the front. I could never get it even at the top. One day my mother told me to "always start at the beginning and work your way up, then it will turn out right." I didn't know then that she was giving me theological advice. To know that you are more than all the stuff of this world is a great blessing. I remember hearing Carl Sagan, the respected scientist, say "we are star stuff" and thinking: we are so much more than merely star stuff.

Beyond all of my psychology and my physicality is an alien quality that has its own category of reality – the Spirit. That Spirit is my True Self – a self that is so much higher and bigger than anything that can be conceived by the mind. Whenever my life becomes chaotic and hurtful, as our lives always do from time to time, I remember who I really am – a Spirit, a spark of the divine – and that knowledge liberates me from the smallness of the world system. It is power in the best sense of that word – a freeing experience of a self that cannot be destroyed or die. That is what Jesus meant in this saying, and indeed it is a blessing.

Insight 19

*Jesus said, "Blessed is he who came into being before
he came into being. If you become my disciples and listen
to my words, these stones will minister to you. For there are
five trees for you in Paradise which remain undisturbed
summer and winter and whose leaves do not fall. Whoever
becomes acquainted with them will not experience death."*

From the Head ...

This insight addresses our origin and our true nature. Most of us have been taught that we are created from the mud of the earth, or that we evolved from lower life forms. But this insight suggests that something in us, that spark or Spirit, was neither created by God nor evolved from some other earthly life – it was before all things. This Spirit is literally a part of God – the true God beyond all other images and secondary representations of the divine.

Jesus says that the stones will minister to you if you have this knowledge. That is a beautiful way of saying that not even the hardness of the world can be a barrier to real joy that spiritual knowledge brings. Whereas the world system and all its forms are like stones, the world of Light and Spirit is soft, tender and loving.

The idea that there are trees in paradise represents many things. In later Gnostic thinking on the subject, the trees represented spiritual rituals that are used as paths to root oneself into the other reality beyond this world. Trees give shade in the heat of the day, and are life giving and restful. Also, trees represent strength. Jesus says that these trees in paradise are undisturbed by the world, that all the suffering and torment that we feel here does not shake the higher reality from being what it is – the truth beyond.

Again, Jesus brings power and force to his words. "Whoever becomes acquainted with them will not experience death" he says. This world is a world of death – that feeds on itself, but in the world of the Spirit death is not a part of the system, and it has no predatory nature to it. It is undisturbed. Nothing falls off and dies like leaves in the winter, and although the spiritual reality beyond this world is dynamic, it does not destroy through the dynamics of its force and beauty. When this truth is known personally (by gnosis), it liberates us from fear.

From the Heart ...

I grew up in Tulsa, Oklahoma. I lived there until I was about 9 years old. Recently, I went back to visit my old neighborhood – I hadn't been there in 35 years. I discovered that some years back a flood destroyed all of the houses in that area, and where my house once stood was now just an empty lot. It had been washed away. As I stood there on the lot just looking around, I was struck by this insight: "Blessed is he who came into being before he came into being." Something in me is older than all of the world, and no flood or violence done in this world can destroy that origin. In this world everything gets washed away, and vanishes like the wind. Dust and emptiness. But my True Self is older than time itself, and pre-dates the stars.

I walked around that area for awhile. It was a hot summer day, with little or no breeze. I stood under a large tree and just felt my childhood there. The tree was old and, interestingly, it had survived the flood whereas the houses were torn apart. That is the imagery this insight of Jesus casts. I felt a great sense of my own acquaintance with the gnosis (knowledge) that saves at that moment. I was not in grief or terror at the destruction and loss of my childhood home, but just stood in wonderment at the marvel of the Spirit. I was more than my earthly origin.

Insight 20

*The disciples said to Jesus, "Tell us what the
Kingdom of Heaven is like." He said to them,
"It is like a mustard seed. It is the smallest of all seeds.
But when it falls on tilled soil, it produces a great
plant and becomes a shelter for birds of the sky."*

From the Head ...

How does spiritual knowledge begin? It begins in the smallest
ways, with the slightest of questions. It grows and grows, and soon it
becomes everything. That is the way of spirituality. Once it begins
and is tilled and nurtured, it becomes a strong force, and literally
overtakes everything else.

This insight appears in the public Gospels as well, but here the
imagery is a little more elaborate. Spirituality produces a kind of
shelter for us – a place to take refuge amidst the ordeals of the world.
The imagery of the Spirit being a bird of the sky is typical for Jesus
and those who speak of spiritual things. A bird is not stuck to the
ground, but can fly away in times of danger, or can go to the highest
point when the floods come. Thus, a person who is acquainted with
his True Self can take shelter in his knowledge, and seek higher
ground when the hurt of the world threatens.

From the Heart ...

As the seed of my spirituality grew, it began to change everything in
my life. I could no longer just look at the world the way I once did –
unconsciously and without question. Sure, for a very long time I

thought I was spiritual. But I wasn't – not really. I was just going through the motions, acting. But, there came a time when my acting didn't work for me. I had to either step out of my role-playing life, or lose myself to it all the more. The "normal" routine of life eats spirituality, but suddenly as I tilled it and nurtured it, it grew into a large plant that shaded me from everything else. The mustard seed had grown.

With the seed grown, I just flew away. I became a bird – unstuck to my previous roles. In a real sense, the Spirit grew wings in me. Was I crazy? Of course! The normal rules didn't apply to me anymore. Why would they? Do the birds stop at our stop lights? Or, do they work in our factories? That's ridiculous. For a time, I laughed at just about everything, because it seemed just so silly. Weird little birds are we, who hop upon the ground not realizing we have wings to soar with.

Insight 21

> *Mary said to Jesus, "Whom are your disciples like?"*
> *He said, "They are like children who have settled in a*
> *field which is not theirs. When the owners of the field come,*
> *they will say, 'Let us have back our field.' They will undress*
> *in their presence in order to let them have back their field*
> *and to give it back to them. Therefore I say, if the owner*
> *of a house knows that the thief is coming, he will begin his*
> *vigil before he comes and will not let him dig through into*
> *his house of his domain to carry away his goods. You then,*
> *be on your guard against the world. Arm yourselves with*
> *great strength lest the robbers find a way to come to you,*
> *for the difficulty which you expect will surely materialize.*
> *Let there be among you a man of understanding. When*
> *the grain ripened, he came quickly with his sickle in his*
> *hand and reaped it. Whoever has ears to hear, let him hear."*

From the Head ...

First thing that strikes me about this insight is that it is in response to a question from Mary – a disciple of Jesus who is not recognized as such in the public Gospels. Only in Gnostic Gospels are women recognized as disciples of Jesus and given a place of honor. She is treated with seriousness and regard. Her question is thoroughly answered by Jesus.

For Gnostics, among whom I place Jesus, regarded women as representing the Spirit. They tended to revere Eve instead of blaming her for beguiling Adam, who is usually seen as representing the soul. So, the issue of whether women should be counted as disciples of Jesus is not even addressed here – it is assumed.

Jesus' answer to Mary's question reveals his understanding of the world as utter darkness. His disciples are children who will undress themselves and give their bodies to the world as they return to their heavenly home in the Spirit. How seductive the world is in convincing us that we are merely flesh and blood and children of the earth. We are on one level, but on another, we are alien from this plane of existence.

The world is predatory. Be on your guard. These are Jesus' warnings. The world will reap your consciousness if it can – like a sickle being flung against the wheat.

There is a deep cutting edge to Jesus' teachings. He is not soft pedaling the darkness, nor teaching a positive thinking theology about the world. The world, in Jesus' words, is against you – your Spirit. It is a trap meant to devour your true essence, and feed on its life force, and then throw you back into it and re-plant you. This cycle is stopped only when we stop it through knowing who we truly are, and moving our awareness into appropriate activity. Jesus, as usual, asks us to really pay attention. Listen! For we have responsibility for our own Spirit.

From the Heart ...

Most of my life I have repeated the same mistakes over and over. There is a kind of force that compels us to do so, and we each fall prey to this force until we deliberately and with intent move away from it. I never really paid attention to it until it almost killed me by sucking the energy from me like a vampire on some lonely street late at night. Seem over dramatic? It's not. Our awareness is consumed systematically by the world. Our Spirit is the seed of this awareness and a great prize (the pearl of great price!), and thus it is the battleground over which the forces collide.

How do these forces collide? We see it everyday, but don't pay the slightest bit of attention. Lulled into sleep we follow like sheep. We are kept emotional in our relationships, entertained with our sports, and fascinated by sex, drugs and the consuming process. We don't see, and we stop wanting to see. Religion is the greatest enemy of Spirit, with simple answers and simple recipes for living that don't force one to ask the hard questions and look at what's really happening to them.

I hate to admit it, but I was truly a part of all these forces. Still am, as are you. They swirl around us all the time, and it is so easy to get caught up in them. Our families get us locked into a rat race; our desire gets us trapped into sexual intrigue. Our thirst for excitement ventures us into actions not worthy of our Spirit. Be on your guard against the world! Wake up, and pay attention. That is Jesus' advice. Its so hard to take, because it seems so dark, and we hate to see the darkness.

But the important thing, I suppose, is that above and beyond all the darkness is something far richer and greater. To possess that knowledge is to drop fear to the side, and "undress" in the world, and lay the suffering aside. That is what I try to remember. It is an insight worth remembering.

Insight 22

Jesus saw infants being suckled. He said to his disciples, "These infants being suckled are like those who enter the kingdom." They said to him, "Shall we then, as children, enter the kingdom?" Jesus said to them, "When you make the two one, and when you make the inside like the outside and the outside like the inside, and the above like the below and when you make the male and the female one and the same, so that the male not be male nor the female female; and when you fashion eyes in place of an eye, and a hand in place of a hand, and a foot in place of a foot, and a likeness in place of a likeness; then will you enter the kingdom."

From the Head ...

The first part of this insight is familiar. It appears in the public Gospels, although in a bit different form. The rest of this saying is remarkable in that it leads the disciple(s) into seeing how shattered their world is, and how much repair to their way of seeing must be done in order to enter the reality of the Spirit.

Our sense of reality is taught to us. We are educated in the way of our consensual agreements, and those agreements become our collective facts. However, those facts are not truth. Existence creates division, divisions that are more illusory than they are real. Our social structures become based on those divisions, and people are categorized into classes, races and cultures.

Women, for instance, tend to make less money than men. There are social reasons for this difference, and those reasons are based on assumptions derived from the divisions within the world. When our secondary structures and institutions make qualitative separations, as they do, the split deepens. We become more and more alienated from one another.

Jesus is teaching a way of seeing that dissolves the shattering. Physical difference is not important – respect for the Spirit is. When you come to respect the Spirit underneath, the walls between people cease to exist, and the shattering that is created by the world is overcome. Perception is a key factor in this insight. How do we see? What do we see? Where are we standing when we see what we see? These are internal questions that have to be asked as we move from the Kingdom of Darkness into the Kingdom of Light.

From the Heart ...

When my son was a toddler he did strange things like talk to trees, or say good-bye to the house when we left it. When he got tired, he ... lay down and slept. He had no rules about all this. Over time, of course, we began the process of training him – where to sleep, how to eat, what to talk to, and where to go to the bathroom. Very normal stuff. But I realized that while we were teaching him, he was losing something in the process. Reality to him was fluid and not fixed at all, but we were teaching him our reality, and it was very fixed and concrete. Soon, he stopped talking to trees and saying good-bye to the house. He stopped touching the face of strangers he would meet, because we had taught him the dangers, and educated him as to what was correct behavior, and what was not.

To enter the kingdom that Jesus is talking about doesn't mean that you have to ignore the dangers and pitfalls of the world. It does mean that you have to look differently at everything. You have to begin to see spiritually. Perhaps that's what little children do naturally.

Another thing that strikes me about this insight is just how vulnerable children are. As I moved away from the normality of ordinary seeing, I felt very fragile and vulnerable, too. Sometimes I felt just like a little kid going to school for the first time, separated from everything I had known. But it was that same vulnerability that helped me see differently.

I remember the story of Adam in the Garden of Eden, who after having eaten from the Tree of Knowledge, saw his own nakedness. In orthodox thinking, that was the moment of the "Fall," but from this point of view, it is the moment of awakening. In the awakening, of course, you begin to see that all the comfort that was felt before, was just false comfort – that in truth, to live unaware is to be the most vulnerable of all.

False comfort and false divisions are features that need to be overcome in the world of the Spirit. That is what I think Jesus means here, at least in part. It means: to live differently one must see differently. I know that to be a deep truth.

Insight 23

Jesus said, "I shall choose you, one out of a thousand, and two out of ten thousand, and they shall stand as a single one."

From the Head ...

The difficulty of doing spiritual work separates you out of ordinary reality and out of the crowd. Indeed, it feels as though you have been exiled, for in truth you are living in a world of exile, and only those who possess spiritual sight can see it.

This insight is not meant to make someone feel that he or she has been specially "elected" or "foreordained" – chosen by God, while the rest just flounder. What this insight suggests is that those who are doing the work of the Spirit are pulled out of their world by that work, into a different world. The good news is that this new world has a community as well. In more mystical terms, the Light draws itself together.

Jesus was realistic about the difficulty of this work. Few choose to do it. Most take what they deem to be the softer, easier way. In fact, of course, the ease of ordinary reality is illusory. There is nothing harder than being in the world. It is hell. So, the hard work of the Spirit is really the place of repose, as the Gnostic Gospels universally assert, while remaining in the world is the real difficulty. But only those who do the work of the Spirit begin to see this truth. It is one of those conundrums that makes spiritual talk so difficult.

From the Heart ...

A friend came to me just after I had made the decision to change my life, and told me that I needed to see a counselor. As a therapist for many years, I could see that my friend was really bothered by my decision, and I asked him why he thought that I needed help. He said that what I was doing was crazy. "How are you going to make a living? What will you do? Where will you live?" He was, of course, projecting his fears onto me. I told him that I felt very secure and wasn't worried. He just shook his head. I never saw him again.

So many of our friendships are based upon the circle of our lives. When we break that circle, those friendships end – they just evaporate because they have no context anymore. They are shallow friendships, with no real substance or depth. True friendships are more like authentic kinship. The context is unimportant. Whether it is in a work place or a vacation spot, it doesn't matter. Whether you fit in or not, that, too, doesn't matter. My friends that were involved with the Spirit understood – perhaps not entirely, but in ways that did not even need to be spoken of.

There is a story in the public Gospels about Jesus' Mother coming to see him after he started his ministry. He said "Who is my Mother? Who are my brothers and sisters? Whoever hears my words are my Mother, my brothers and sisters." He wasn't being negative about his Mother, but he was making a point. That is exactly how it feels. You feel pulled out of the ordinary world of things, but then you come to something beyond it. Maybe that's what Jesus meant here.

Insight 24

His disciples said to him, "Show us the place where you are, since it is necessary for us to seek it." He said to them, "Whoever has ears, let him hear. There is light within a person of light, and that person lights up the whole world. If that person does not shine, that person is darkness."

From the Head ...

This insight is a great deal different from the same story that is told in the public Gospels. In the public story Jesus is said to have told the disciples: "I am the Truth and the life, no one comes to the father but by me." But here, Jesus turns the reference point onto the disciples themselves. He tells them in essence, find the light within yourselves and go there. That is where you need to stand. That is where you will know all that you need to know.

Jesus' sayings, according to Thomas' recordings, do not lend themselves to control of people. Perhaps one of the major reasons this book was pushed away from the canon was that it gave people too much individual power to seek truth. The individual, not the church, would be the final source of spiritual reality.

People look for external authority to guide them. Ordinary religions use this need to control people, and justify it to themselves as "comforting the masses." In this insight Jesus is pushing the disciples to look within themselves for guidance – to find that inner light. For if that light is not found, they become the darkness themselves, he is saying.

In another Gnostic work of the early era, "The Dialogue of the Savior," where Jesus literally discusses spiritual issues with his disciples, this same question comes up. In that work it says: "They said to him, 'What is the place to which we are going?' The Lord said, 'Stand in the place you can reach!'" (Nag Hammadi Library, vs. 77 & 78) Once again, the difference between the secret teachings and the orthodox Gospels is obvious. Little wonder that people have refused to take responsibility for their own spirituality, and blindly followed authority into the darkness of crusades, witch burning and inquisitions.

From the Heart ...

My parents were not religious people. I use to go to church by myself when I was young. It fascinated me, and drew on my sense that there was something more than just this world of ordinariness. But even as a child the harshness of the Bible belt preaching didn't make sense to something inside of me, and one day I just stopped going. Later on I was told that those things that I found troublesome just needed to be taken on "faith," and that I needed to trust. I tried to do that, but my inner knowledge haunted me.

The more I learned, the more I realized that my inner wisdom and intuition were right. Blind faith in authority was a darkness, and in giving yourself over to that authority you become the darkness as well.

When I was in college I was accustomed to running into people handing out religious tracts on campus. They would hand them out, and occasionally talk with you if you were so disposed. My encounters with these people always left me feeling that they were vacant inside of any real authentic acknowledgement of the human condition. They had simply hidden inside a doctrine to alleviate their fear. Most zealous religious fever strikes me this way.

Religiosity leads to robotic living and simplistic answers. No heart. No passion for truth. Just blind obedience. There is an old hymn that says it all: "Trust and Obey" – that is real darkness! I refuse to be a good little robot for the system.

Insight 25

Jesus said, "Love your brother like your soul, guard him like the pupil of your eye."

From the Head ...

This saying, like many of Jesus' teachings, has a dual meaning. The obvious meaning is rather straightforward: take care of your spiritual brothers and sisters. Help them understand and guard them against pitfalls. In other words, be there for them. Jesus' commandment to "love one another" is not, actually, unique to him or to spiritual teachers in general. However, he repeatedly reinforces this admonition, since loving is such an essential spiritual quality.

The less obvious meaning has to do with the symbolism of the Spirit and the Soul, which are seen as brothers. The Soul, which comes forth out of the world matrix of psychological and mental factors, needs the total reflection of the Spirit behind it for it to have the quality needed to traverse the world. Our soul stuff is rather obvious to most of us. We guard ourselves through an elaborate array of defense mechanisms, meant to shield us from the terror of life. What we commonly do not do, however, is guard our Spirit with the same zealousness. We can guard our soul, and give our Spirit over to the world – this is the path of darkness. By ignoring the soul's brother (or sister – the Spirit is usually understood as feminine) the soul remains lost and without hope. An awakened Spirit aids the soul, and in turn the soul guards the Spirit as one would guard a dear loved one.

The pupil of the eye has special significance, since the pupil is the opening through which light enters. The Spirit is the light, or the spark, as it is often termed in Gnostic thought. The soul is very much like the pupil in that it is through the soul that the light shines forth.

To do soul work, which is a strengthening of the soul for its task of revealing the true light of the Spirit, is critical to Jesus' teachings. Soul work has to do with perception, intent, and attention. The soul is an energy force, which is sometimes called the energy body. It can be aided and strengthened, or it can be damaged and even destroyed. The Spirit, on the other hand, cannot be destroyed by this world, but it can be kept "asleep" and unable to reveal itself when the soul is damaged or destroyed. Significant soul work loosens the hold the world has on the Spirit, and allows the Spirit to eventually escape the suffering and material/energy process of existence, and return to its true spiritual reality.

This teaching has a great deal of power for those within the inner circle of knowledge that Jesus is speaking to. He is reminding them of the constant need for awareness. This awareness is the greatest guard against the enemy of the Spirit, which is the dark depression of the world that seeks to keep it enslaved to the material/energy processes. This short insight packs a punch.

From the Heart ...

Dear "spiritual" friends are those that will see when you are in a deep soul work time, building strength for the great work of revealing Spirit. I had several such friends, and they were invaluable in guarding me against slipping and falling away from what was really happening in my life. They offered no false comfort, nor easy answers. They just stood by with love and gentle guidance when necessary. I have served that purpose in many people's lives myself, and it is a great honor. It wasn't easy to let them in to see what was happening to me, although they could see it without my acknowledgement.

For me, I had to work on intent – to stay focused with what I was really about as a person of Spirit. My perception had brought me to a certain point in my life. I had paid attention to the prompting that activated and stirred my Spirit, but it was intent that became critical. My friends guarded me like the pupil of their eye, so I could stay aware, and not fall prey to fear, false demands and the role play of the ordinary world.

I was in a world of dual conflicts: the ones inside, and the ones outside. They rush at each other like giant waves crashing together to form a storm. The birthing of my Spirit was exactly that – a birth of something from beyond the scope of the world. I came to understand what Jesus meant when he spoke of a "second birth" – not in the sense that is ordinarily understood by orthodox religions as a simple believing of something or something that is symbolic in nature. No! This was not symbolic. The birth was a literal coming forth. Now, I sense its presence within, alive and awake to itself. I guard it like the pupil of my eye.

Insight 26

> Jesus said, "You see the mote in your brother's eye,
> but you do not see the beam in your own eye. When you
> cast the beam out of your own eye, then you will see
> clearly to cast the mote from your brother's eye."

From the Head ...

Again, this insight is similar to the one in the public Gospels. It builds on Jesus' teaching of non-judgmental living. We tend to make morality and consensual behavior the focus of our religious beliefs, and ignore the deeper issue of who we are. Judgmentalism is a way we externalize ourselves. In the public Gospels Jesus asks, "What does it profit a man to gain the whole world at the loss of his True Self?" We each know the answer to this timeless question, and yet we repeatedly make judgments that keep us away from our deeper inner reality. The example that Jesus gives has a kind of humor to it that makes it easy to see the issue. How can you see a splinter in someone's eye when there is a log in your own eye?

Another aspect of this insight is also relevant: that we internally judge ourselves. Inside of us are many characteristics and features. As Freud and other modern thinkers discovered, we have component parts that function in critical relationship to one another. They are "brothers" to each other, but act independently. Consequently, we judge ourselves as if we are independent of ourselves. We do a certain thing, and then another part of us judges that behavior as wrong. We build up guilt and shame, and our inner conflict creates anxiety in everything we do. Freud saw this as a conflict between inner drives; between the Id and the Super Ego – the battleground being the Ego itself.

From the Heart . . .

My father, who died when I was in high school, lived a very disciplined life built around work. To work and make money was his primary function, and that was the way he lived. I'm not sure I ever saw him truly relaxed. I mention this because I discovered that my father was in my head as I was attempting to break free of ordinary reality. I started to feel guilty and strange, like I was doing something wrong, and I should feel bad. It took me a while to identify the force inside, but sure enough it was my father's face that kept sneaking in. He would have never approved of such behavior.

I dealt with this by simply going into the bathroom one afternoon and staring into the mirror. I addressed him as if he actually lived in me. I told him he had no business there anymore, and that he was to get out. I told him that my Spirit was in charge, not him. I affirmed my love for him, but I was resolved. It worked! I felt relieved that I had gained my freedom through my awareness and attention to the issue.

For, the issue of being externally judgmental was not nearly as great as the issue of being internally judgmental. This insight helped me have humor with myself, and yet keep the attention focused on what I needed to do.

Insight 27

> *Jesus said, "If you do not fast as regards the world, you will not find the kingdom. If you do not observe the Sabbath as a Sabbath, you will not see the father."*

From the Head ...

Fasting is a common practice of sacrifice that is meant to deepen the spiritual life of the person. Generally speaking, fasting is the abstaining from food, sometimes food and drink, for a prescribed period of time. The intent of the fast is to turn away from the body's need so that one might attend to the need of the Spirit.

In this insight, Jesus is saying that fasting with regard to the world itself is required. It is not a matter of avoiding certain foods, or even all foods for a period of time, but rather the abstaining from the world's power and force – its seductive influence on the Spirit. Many might think this "fasting" requires a monastic life – being removed from day to day living in the world. But that is not what Jesus is teaching here. A person may fast, and yet be around food. It depends on the person's inner discipline as to whether that is possible, or whether it is necessary to separate oneself from the temptation to eat in whatever manner necessary.

The world has a seductive power that feeds on the Spirit, so to fast with regard to the world is actually depriving the world of its source of food. When a person deprives the world of its meaningfulness and his or her attention, the world shrinks in its ability to control and hold the Spirit in bondage. This practice of fasting is the true Sabbath.

In Gnostic mythology on the subject, the Spirit "falls" into the world and sleeps to its true nature by eating of the food of the world, and clothing itself in the world's skin. To fast is to literally stop the assault on the Spirit, through remembering the true source of being and one's true essence. This insight is an act of remembrance, quite literally an avenue of remembering the truth of one's self.

From the Heart ...

A few years ago I decided that I needed to spend some time away from the normal routine of my life. I made an agreement with myself that I would go to a place and not talk to anybody for at least a week. I took no books to read, no tapes to listen to – nothing that might divert me from being with myself. I had never done anything like that in my life. True, I had gone on vacations where I was relatively secluded, but this was not the same.

After just a couple of days I thought I would go crazy if I didn't have something to do, or someone to talk to. It was just sheer will power that kept me from going to a movie, or seeking someone out – if only to order food from them. It was harder than I thought it would be. It took about 5 days for me to get some clarity and just really be with myself. After that, I was struck with what actually came to me. I began to see differently, and intuited things that were of importance to my life. It was during this time that I had what can only be called a mystical experience – a vision that I will not attempt to explain.

I was not trying to have this experience. I was just simply trying to empty myself of the junk of the world – the noise and distractions that surround us every day. I discovered that an experience like this cannot occur unless I fasted from the world – an act of deliberate quieting of all pre-conceived reality. I believe Carlos Castaneda called this: "stopping the world." This is what Jesus called "the Sabbath."

The Sabbath is not a gathering into a church for religious talk, nor is it a day set aside for religious ritual. It is a deliberate act of fasting from the ordinary reality of the world, and placing oneself in that neutral place where the world stops and the Spirit is experienced.

Insight 28

Jesus said, "I took my place in the midst of the world, and I appeared to them in flesh. I found all of them intoxicated; I found none of them thirsty. And my soul became afflicted for the sons of men, because they are blind in their hearts and do not have sight; for empty they came into the world, and empty too they seek to leave the world. But for the moment they are intoxicated. When they shake off their wine, then they will repent."

From the Head ...

The Buddha sat under the Bodhi tree until he opened his eyes and said: I am awake! Jesus, likewise, awakened in the midst of the world and saw the ignorance that is intoxication with the world of matter. The bondage of the Spirit in the world is painful – an affliction.

This insight has to do with the role of redeemer. In later Gnostic thinking on the subject, the Redeemer, who is an awakener of the Spirit, comes into the world to perform the specific task of bringing the Spirit out of its ignorance and sleep. Although Jesus was this redeemer, for Gnostics all others who awaken to their true nature became redeemers as well. The most basic task of the redeemer is not to save people from sin or some wrongdoing, but to remind them of who they really are – children of the Light.

The world is a place of emptiness and darkness, and it "blinds" the Spirit as to its true identity. Coming into the world is an act of emptiness itself – a dark abyss that the ancient Gnostics saw as a hellish trap. Salvation from this hellish trap is awakening to the truth of self.

Repentance in this sense, is simply knowing who you truly are beyond the confusion and false passions of the world system.

Notice the lack of atonement theology here. Jesus does not need to die for sins, because the world itself is viewed as a kind of death. The world is intoxication, sleep, anguish and death – all false realities that lay claim to the Spirit, but in fact have no real power in and of themselves. Upon awakening, this truth is known (gnosis) and the world is overcome through this act of self-knowledge.

This insight, which at first reading seems to be about Jesus, is actually about each of us. We come to understand that each of us is the redeemer, and our only true job in this world is the liberation of the Spirit from its bondage.

From the Heart ...

It occurred to me how serious it is to take on the role of redeemer in one's life. To do so, one must walk as a liberator in all things. That is easier said than done. Life here in this world is a mess. We experience that "mess" frequently, and it causes us great suffering and confusion. We are told that if we just believed right things, and acted in correct ways, everything will work out for the best. That, of course, is a lie. Nothing ever works out. It may appear to, but that "working out" really just works us in – not out at all.

If this seems dark it is because it is dark. The first act of awakening is always brutal honesty. Most people don't want to get this honest about their lives. They like believing in their illusions, even though somewhere they know the truth. This inner truth is hard to awaken – ignorance is stubborn.

I often think about my own stubbornness. How long did it take for me to admit the truth of the world in which I found myself? I was incessantly trying to explain things to myself that would make it all work out. I would try hard to force rationality onto something that made no sense at all. All meaningfulness I found in the world was projected meaningfulness. It took me awhile to discover that insight.

As I awakened to my True Self, I discovered that I was not afraid of suffering. I was not afraid to sit with people going through terrible things, for I knew that the horror of it all was not the truth of them, but of the world around them. That distinction made a great difference to me. I could see their inner beauty – their inner perfection – caught in a swamp of muddy water. To be sure, our actions make matters worse – no doubt about it. But ultimately I saw that the world itself was the matrix of conflict that created such behavior. This did not excuse irresponsibility or hurtfulness on the part of individuals – for some have become so allied with the darkness that they have become the darkness itself. But, it did give me a way of being with people that helped me be an advocate for their True Self, and not all the junk that goes on around and through us.

The statement, "I am the light that surpasses the world" is one of true enlightenment. To walk that talk is the task of the redeemer. It became my task, as it must for each of us.

Insight 29

> Jesus said, "If the flesh came into being because of Spirit, it is a wonder. But if Spirit came into being because of the body, it is a wonder of wonders. Indeed, I am amazed at how this great wealth has made its home it this poverty."

From the Head ...

Although this sounds like a chicken or the egg argument, it isn't. The operative word here is "being" – for the Spirit , presumably the redeemer, comes into being (in the world) to awaken those who slumber here. The idea that the Spirit is in exile plays a large part in this saying. Imagine, to make this idea a bit more understandable, a wealthy Prince who is exiled into a foreign land. After a time the Prince loses his sense of identity, and becomes enmeshed in the poverty of the foreign country, and sees himself as being a part of that world. Then, one day, an emissary from the Prince's true home is sent to bring him back. Upon seeing the Prince the emissary is sad and amazed at how the Prince has lost himself in the web of the exiled world. It is the emissary's task to awaken the Prince to his true identity, and bring him back home. The Prince may not believe that he is the Prince, and think that it is a trick to hurt him. He may even be angry at the emissary, and accuse him of falseness and lies. At any rate, the awakening to the truth is never an easy one.

People believe themselves to be created out of the mud, or to have come from lower species. And to be sure, this is the case with a great deal of our make-up. However, that inner spark is not made of the stuff of this world. At first hearing it sounds strange and weird – like a peasant being told he is actually a Prince caught in forgetfulness. But this insight suggests that this is the case, as do all of Jesus' "secret teachings." As with all insights, it takes awhile for this issue to sink in. People respond either in awakening or anger – it is impossible to be dispassionate about such a claim. That is the burden carried by the redeemer(s).

From the Heart ...

What do I believe about myself, and why do I believe it? Does the inner voice conflict with what I believe about myself and the world? Good questions. They certainly became my questions for a long time.

After reading the Gospel of Thomas I was forced to search myself and make some determinations about who I was as a being in this world. Was my discomfort a product of some psychological malady that could be resolved, or was it deeper than that? This insight, and the entire Gospel, brought that question to a head for me. Who was I really? The answer to that question would dictate how I walked through the world, and how I would think about it. Was I really the child of a world whose wonder and glory was so magnificent that I couldn't imagine it or remember it? Or, was this world my home and my longing just a part of what it meant to be a person? We each, whether we take conscious responsibility for it or not, answer these questions. I began to know the truth of what this insight suggested. That became my answer, and changed everything.

Insight 30

Jesus said, "Where there are three gods, they are gods. Where there are two or one, I am with him."

From the Head ...

Some scholars have suggested that this saying is corrupted, that is, it is a mistranslation of the early Greek text which says that "where there are three, they are without God." In that case, it is most certainly a rejection of the need for community (here symbolized by the number three). It therefore is an anti-institutional saying, suggesting that only a solitary individual can experience God. I am not certain this is the case.

The other possibility is that this saying is accurately transcribed by Thomas, and Jesus is suggesting the multi-imaged nature of how the divine is envisioned. The mythological imagery surrounding a divine revelation, this insight says, matters less than seeing the wholeness of the Spirit behind it.

Many religious forms, specifically Hinduism and Gnosticism, make use of mythological imagery in abundance to express the vastness of the Spirit beyond all hardened forms. This insight might make reference to the fact that people often confuse the image(s) of divine revelation with the revelation itself. In other words, we tend to mix the vehicle with the passenger riding in the vehicle. Someone who has parked their car in a parking lot might say, "Where am I parked?" Well, they are not parked at all, but their car is parked. This happens with religious understandings as well. Thus, religions can become, as they inevitably do, fixated on their own presentation of revelation, thinking that it is identical with the revelation itself.

This error in perception creates tension between religious forms that need not be problematic. All religions have some truth, all have some error. The more a religion takes its imagery to be "the only way" the more error it creates. Jesus is certainly aware of this situation and makes use of it here as a teaching tool. It doesn't matter, he seems to be saying, whether there are many forms of a divine revelation or a single one – I (the divine presence) am there.

From the Heart ...

Religion is one of those issues where everyone thinks he's right. However, it is obvious to most thoughtful people that no one form has a hold on the truth. I began to see great value in forms of religious expression and imagery that were not familiar to me. I had always thought that, but never really explored in depth religions that seemed culturally alien to my own. As I took seriously the idea that the divine presents itself in a multiplicity of ways, I began to see the in-breaking of the Spirit in many ways I had never thought of. Frankly, I was surprised I hadn't seen it earlier, but the truth was I wasn't awake enough to see.

The more awake you are the more you see the Spirit trying hard to awaken people. It is all around us, and yet we do not see. I realized in this way, that although the Spirit in me was living an exiled life, it was not abandoned here without aid in its struggle to return home. Everywhere I looked I began to see the effort of the Spirit to aid me. Wow! I never realized how dense I was.

Insight 31

> *Jesus said, "No prophet is accepted*
> *in his own village; no physician*
> *heals those who know him."*

From the Head ...

Again, this saying is familiar. It appears in the public Gospels as well. It also has a parallel in the sayings of the Buddha. The source of this saying is universal wisdom.

As we grow up people around us form opinions and ideas of who we are. Those ideas begin to define us, and it is literally impossible to shake them. Like someone who gets stuck with a nickname which follows him the rest of his life – unless he moves away to another town where no one knows who he is. This definition of our self that is given to us by our peers and family shapes how we are viewed and determines whether we are to be respected, taken seriously, or dismissed as a fool. Whatever the case, its power is obvious.

Carlos Castaneda's Don Juan suggests "erasing personal history" as a way to overcome this dilemma – which is simply never telling anyone your past or where you are from. After all, we grow up having faults and making mistakes as anyone does. Upon awakening, who we were is basically erased. It no longer matters, and that person is not us anymore. We speak and move from a different place within ourselves, although we may externally look the same.

Jesus had this problem, as others have. Other people's definition of us doesn't change easily, and it is a battle not worthy of our effort. It is difficult enough to have changed our own inner definitions based on those external ones. In the public Gospels it tells us that Jesus barely escaped his home town with his life. That is how powerful this early definition is. That is why enlightened and awakened people rarely stay around their home town. The fight against the definitional power is just too strong a force to contend with. It is best to move along.

From the Heart ...

People have a way of seeing you that put you into a certain box. As you become aware of your True Self, this box closes in and tries to keep you in check. It isn't pleasant. The definition that people form of us is all part of the social consensual reality that holds us in bondage to the world systems. To waken will literally require a move. Sometimes, more often than not, it requires a move away from family and old friends. Sometimes it requires a divorce or estrangement from family circles. Why? Because the definition of the old self is always overlaid upon you, and the conflict is so immense as to create a needless battle ground.

For me this meant a move and a more private lifestyle. It meant becoming inaccessible except to those that I chose to be with. That may sound harsh, but I found it to be quite necessary. The world seeks to define you. That is how it controls. The awakened person is always beyond definition.

Insight 32

> *Jesus said, "A city being built on a high mountain and fortified cannot fall, nor can it be hidden."*

From the Head ...

This analogy would have been very clear to the people of Jesus' time. Cities were often fortified against invasion, but the strongest of them were also the most obvious. Thus it is with the Spirit, he is saying, for as you strengthen it, its life becomes very obvious.

The theme of "fortifying" your Spirit is a common one in these insights. Since the state of the Spirit in this world is one of sleep and intoxication, to fortify the awakened Spirit is to keep a watch over it at all times and to ensure that it does not go back to sleep or drink from the wine of this world that will make it drunk with attachment. Much like a city that expects attacks from foreign invaders, guards are posted around the clock. Awareness, attention and intention are bulwarks of the fortified Spirit.

It is a dangerous world – that is the point. The difference between this approach and that of many others, is that it takes quite seriously the darkness of the world. The world is not a learning laboratory where the Spirit comes to get a kind of spiritual education. If fact, the greatest enemy of the Spirit is the "hardness" of the world that holds it in place – like quicksand engulfing it as it sinks. The only lesson, if you can call it that, is release – the ability to let go and detach from the pressure and blind process of the world system. Everything else is just illusory, since the process itself has a dark intent to enslave.

What this means is that the more awakened a Spirit becomes, the more under attack it is likely to find itself. The "gravity" of the system is a kind of pressure to keep the Spirit attached to the world, since the world cannot survive without it. Liberation of the Spirit is death to the blind process of the world. That which makes the system work, also makes it seek the Spirit as a "food" source. So, Jesus insists that this situation be taken into account at all times. To deny this is literally to put the Spirit in jeopardy.

From the Heart . . .

Guarding one's spiritual awakening cannot be emphasized too much. It seemed to me that the more awake I became, the more everything sought to reel me back in. This was true both externally and internally. I found myself needing to be attentive and watchful, so that I didn't just slip back into old patterns, thoughts and behaviors. How easy it is to just "play the game," thinking: so what – it makes no difference. But the difference is huge, and only the awakened Spirit and soul can observe the difference.

One of the things that occurred to me was that we are involved in a cosmic "hide and seek" situation. The true intent of the world is hidden. It seeks to hold. The need of the Spirit is liberation, and yet it must disguise it's intention in order for that liberation to take place. You learn to use the energy of the system – kind of like psychic Judo: instead of blocking punches, you just pull them by you without absorbing the impact.

Guarding and honoring the Spirit are actions that were entirely unfamiliar to me. Maintaining the necessary focus required a skill I had not learned, even through all the discipline I had achieved in school and work. Much is made these days of being a spiritual warrior, and it is true; to be a person of Spirit you also have to become a warrior to keep that Spirit well cared for and tended. It must become everything, for nothing, and I mean nothing else, matters at all.

Insight 33

Jesus said, "Preach from your housetops that which you will hear in your ear. For no one lights a lamp and puts it under a bushel, nor does he put it in a hidden place, but rather he sets it on a lampstand so that everyone who enters and leaves will see its light."

From the Head ...

Again, this is a familiar teaching. It has the obvious meaning of not hiding who you truly are. In other words, walk your talk, and live your truth. But like all of Jesus' teachings, especially in his more private and secret sayings, there is a another meaning as well.

Moving something that you hear into your thinking is critical to spiritual awakening. "Preach from your housetops that which you hear in your ear" refers not just to the act of revealing the message of the Spirit to others, but in bringing it into your mind and allowing it to be shouted to the entirety of yourself: knowing what you know throughout your entire being. The idea is to not isolate your spiritual knowledge into any one aspect or feature of who you are.

The next part of this insight is interesting, because although Jesus says that "no one lights a lamp and puts it under a bushel," that is exactly what has happened to the Spirit. It is kept underneath and hidden. What Jesus means, of course, is that no one who desires the light hides the light; only the person who wants to hide in the shadows will bury the light.

On an even deeper level, this saying has to do with the Spirit's journey out of this world. Entering and leaving the world is now illuminated. The world of light from which the Spirit is born has illuminated the pathway out of the darkness. Everyone who enters and leaves will see the light guiding the way. There is always a great deal of imagery around the movement from darkness into the light – and Jesus is painting a picture of a corridor between the worlds that the Spirit must travel.

The idea of light guiding the way, illuminating the path, is both metaphorical and literal to Jesus. It is metaphorical in that light is understood as the development of the connection between the soul and the Spirit. It is literal in the sense that Jesus is literally doing his work, as all spiritual luminaries must, of illuminating the light itself. The teachings themselves are this lighting of the light.

From the Heart ...

At a minister's meeting one time I had the audacity to suggest preaching should be "truth telling." I said that perhaps what is lacking in churches is simply the honest truth about what our real doubts, feeling and issues were, and so people distrusted the clergy because they sensed a basic dishonesty about the whole thing. Preaching, I went on, seemed to be more about convincing others about what we ourselves doubt or, more often than not, just entertainment – Sunday claptrap for the church-going crowd. The response was defensive, and the suggestion was made that faith, not truth, was the central focus of preaching anyway. People want to believe that something is solid out there, was the general opinion, and after all, if you were to get up there and really talk about the issue of truth from a completely honest point of view, you'd never make your mortgage payments. That was the last minister's meeting I ever went to.

Sadly, I discovered that the ministers were right. People rarely want truth, for when truth is told – as a way of authentic seeking – people run like crazy. Church, as I found out, was really about church, and everything else was just incidental.

The primary issue for me became not just to "preach from the housetops what I (heard) in my ear" as Jesus begins in this insight, but also to become my truth. Doing truth and being truth are two separate things, like doing writing and being a writer: one is just an activity, the other an identity.

How does one become the truth and not hide the light under a bushel basket? I've addressed this in previous insights, but specifically here I sense that it is about an identity issue – the essence of who I am. On this issue I have struggled greatly, as I suppose we all must.

As I awakened to myself as Spirit, I realized how much I was hiding not only from others, but from myself. When I told the ministers that preaching should be about "truth telling" I didn't realize I was really preaching to myself at that point. I was the one living a lie – I had no business trying to instruct others how they should be. The real issue was my own light buried deeply within. It was time for it to be revealed.

Insight 34

*Jesus said, "If a blind man leads a blind man,
they will both fall into a pit."*

From the Head ...

This is a graphic image – two blind people walking, one leading the other. They both fall into a pit and get hurt. Jesus saw that most religious leaders were, as he said in his public teachings, "blind guides" – just as he is saying here. But this insight has a deeper meaning as well.

What makes us blind? That is the question behind the teaching. The answer is: the world itself, with all its desires, forces and attractions. The world blinds us to our spiritual reality. With this understanding then, you cannot look to the world for answers to the spiritual questions of being, which means, you cannot see the divine reality of the true God in the processes and features of this world. For sight to be fostered it must come from the source beyond this world.

All our psychological and physical information is basically erroneous in terms of the truth about who we really are. If we look for information as to our identity there, we will be lead into false realities and limited understanding. So often we confuse our psychological self with our True Self, and it leads us away from authentic knowledge into the illusion of knowledge. Most religious understandings have fallen into this trap, as have most philosophical approaches. The blind leading the blind.

Gnosis is revelatory in nature. It is revealed and not discovered. It is given as a gift, not found as a prize. It is given to the "worthy," which means it is given to those who are truly open to receiving it. Most of us

84

aren't. We are caught up in our attractions and desires, which blind us to anything deeper and beyond the scope of the objectified world.

Jesus, in this insight, is teaching about this most difficult situation. We are in a blind world seeking sight from the blind. Until we stop our seeking and allow the revelation of the Spirit from the alien world to enter into knowing, we are as blind as the world is.

From the Heart ...

What made me blind? Why couldn't I see before, and why could I see so clearly now? Those were questions that often occurred to me. My blindness was caused by my existence itself, and those things that blocked my sight within that existence. The desire for security, comfort and gratification – all hindrances to spiritual awakening. All those things that are natural, are in truth alien to the Spirit, and all those things natural to the Spirit are alien to the world. To see one must literally overturn reality, that is, turn understanding and action upside down.

How was I able to see? The answer to that one came with my exhaustion in the world. After having exhausted all avenues of seeking in the world, I had reached a point where the world no longer mattered to me. At the very moment of thinking that the world no longer held any answers, I was able to allow an answer from beyond the world. It was always there, but I was unavailable to it. That is the nature of revelatory knowledge – it is given, not found.

It was in this time that I discovered the meaning of Jesus' public teaching of "blessed are the poor." To be impoverished in the world is not a matter of money per se, but rather a matter of focus and allegiance. Once you surrender to the utter meaninglessness of life, a world beyond presents itself to you, if you are paying attention. I think I had known this in my head for most of my life, but it wasn't until my heart was "filled with emptiness" that the revelation of something more become apparent. Unexpected sight within the blindness.

Insight 35

Jesus said, "It is not possible for anyone to enter
the house of a strong man and take it by force unless he
binds his hands; then he will be able to ransack his house."

From the Head ...

The strong man's house is the world. It is the residence of the powers that rule the processes of the world. We have entered that house – we were born. How foolish to think that we can do anything to escape without first dealing with the owner of the house: the powers that rule the house. His hands must first be bound, so that one can ransack the house and leave unharmed.

But why ransack the house? What is to be gained? The answer for Jesus was the Spirit itself. Withdrawal of the Spirit from the reality of the world is a ransacking of the house, because it destabilizes what the world feeds upon. It is like siphoning gasoline from an engine. When enough is taken the engine shuts down. In a manner of speaking, that would be ransacking the function of the engine. So it is with the world and the withdrawal of the Spirit. When all is withdrawn, the world will cease.

To bind the hands of the strong man requires strength and surprise. That is what spiritual awakening has on its side. To step aside and not be a part of the consensual agreement that forces compliance to the world's reality is always a surprise. It's crazy, as far as common sense is concerned, but we are not talking about "common sense," we are talking about an extraordinary sense beyond the ordinary.

The house that needs to be ransacked can also be understood as the social reality that is created by the status quo. It confines the Spirit with as much force as does existence itself, since social reality is a direct result of and response to the physical world. To bind the hands of the strong social reality requires a mindful inner force that turns away the desires of the social context in favor of a higher reality. Spiritual discipline is one way of looking at it. Carlos Castaneda called it "stalking." But whatever the terminology, the essential meaning and purpose is the same: freedom for the Spirit.

From the Heart ...

Binding a strong man in his own house conjures up images of violence. To live in the world is a violence against the Spirit, and anyone who is in touch with the Spirit knows the feeling of that violence. It takes dramatic action to bind something as strong as the force of consensual thought with the world. That action feels rather psychically violent to everyone around it, and yet has no obvious target. It is much like watching a person fight a swarm of bees from a distance. He appears to be swatting the wind.

To do the inner work of "fighting the swarm of bees" is unpleasant and uncomfortable. Like so many of the sayings in this collection, this insight touches me where I have a great deal of pain. It was truly a battle for me to "bind the strong man," because at times I just wanted to give in and go along. But that was death, so I was trapped for sure. It was literally fight or die – that is how it felt. The battle for spiritual freedom is never an easy one, nor is it over when you think it is. It goes on and on, and is so hard to get a hold of – like bees swarming around your head, or a strong man in his own house. It is serious business. This insight brings me to that realization quickly, because I am aware of how much I hate conflict. But because I hate it, that is where it presses in the most. The strong man will always punch you where you are the weakest, and the bee will always sting you where you are exposed. This knowledge evades us sometimes.

Insight 36

> *Jesus said, "Do not be concerned from morning until evening and from evening until morning about what you wear."*

From the Head ...

In Gnostic thinking "garment" or "robe" is designation for the body. When a person is said to "take off their garment" they have died. When Jesus says here that we are not to be concerned about what we wear, it is more than simple clothing that he is talking about. He is speaking more specifically about the material body itself.

It isn't surprising that most people concern themselves more with their bodies than they do with their soul or Spirit. The majority of folks "sleep" to their Spirit, and are not the slightest bit aware of the processes of the soul in which the Spirit sleeps. Part of what keeps us asleep is our focus and attention on our material well being.

This insight is not unique to Jesus. All spiritually awakened teachers have taught basically the same thing. In the public Gospels Jesus says: "Where your treasure is, your heart is also;" and then he goes on to say, "Don't be anxious about what you are to eat and drink, and the clothes you will wear." This insight is a re-emphasis of that understanding, but a bit more specific to the body (for which the word "wear" is a metaphor).

Of interest here is also the circular motion of the saying – "from morning until evening and from evening until morning." At first it appears to be a simple statement of not being concerned around the clock, or all the time. But what this insight is driving at is of greater depth. The circular arrangement of the insight also suggests the pattern of re-entrapment of the Spirit from lifetime to lifetime. "Morning to evening" is one lifetime. "Evening to morning" is another, and so forth. This is the predicament of the Spirit in this world – that without the work of the awakening gnosis, the Spirit is trapped over and over again in the process of materiality. The cycle of birth, life, death repeated equals the formulation: morning to evening, evening to morning.

"Do not be concerned" does not mean to do nothing. It means to literally stop worrying about it, and do the necessary work of gnosis to liberate the Spirit from this terrible state of affairs. Those who heard this private insight were aware of its implications, thus it is simple and straightforward.

From the Heart ...

To change one's focus is to change one's attitude, thinking and entire sense of being. That may not be a great insight for some, but for me it was huge. Like all the sayings on the subject of our fixation about this world, it forced me to see just how much I was concerned about who I was perceived as being. That was how I was concerned with what I was "wearing." What that concern was getting me was a re-affirmation of the false reality that makes up the world. It took me a long time to get that.

In the process of awakening, I became aware that I had been here many times before – not only in the same patterns of my life now, but many lifetimes. It wasn't like I could recall specifics, because identity is dissolved by the process each time we are re-invested in the world. But as my Spirit awakened, I became aware of the cycles and gravity that has kept my True Self from escaping over and over again. I had never reached sufficient gnosis to leave the cycle. We become so fixated on the smallness of our lives, we lose touch with the largeness of what is truly occurring. That is one of the "powers" of the world – it changes our focus, and pushes our attention downward into the lower world, instead of upward into the upper world.

This awareness of being "old" was part of the work of gnosis, since the knowledge that something of me – my Spirit – predated everything in this world. That knowledge, or gnosis as I now call it, begins to turn one's focus away from the smallness of the world into the largeness of the Spirit realm. It is a powerful movement within, and in that movement, what concerns you as a being changes drastically.

This simple and short insight of Jesus' which at first seems so apparent and easy, has a kind of edge to it that is often missed unless one sees through spiritual eyes. The development of those "spiritual eyes" is the cornerstone of all gnosis.

Insight 37

*His disciples said, "When will you become
revealed to us and when shall we see you?"
Jesus said, "When you disrobe without
being ashamed and take up your garments
and place them under your feet like little
children and tread on them, then
[will you see] the son of the living one
and you will not be afraid."*

From the Head ...

Only the Spirit can witness the Spirit. The essence of something cannot be viewed until one's own essence is discovered. The discovering of this true essence is much like birth (being a little child) or death (disrobing).

What interests me here is the comment at the end, "and you will not be afraid." It connects to the idea of not "being ashamed." Fear and shame are two very powerful components in our lives. To become unashamed of being different in the world is important to disconnecting from the power of the world. Our families and most of our ordinary friends are "powers" that keep us locked into a definition about ourselves. To move away from that definition is "shameful" to ordinary society. It is crazy. To take off the robe without shame is actually a kind of turning of words, since the real "shame" is having put on the robe in the first place. The real terror is the alien world in which the Spirit finds itself, and yet, we are afraid that to lose the robe of this world is to lose identity. In actual truth, we live in the midst of lost identity, and it is only when we awaken to this realization that we can move from the fear of this world into the peace of the Spirit.

Another point to be made here is the reference to "the son of the living one." The son of the living one is, of course, our True Self – symbolically represented throughout these insights by Jesus himself. The "living one" is the spiritual reality – the true world that is alive, since the world of matter and material is but a shadow that has no real life unto itself.

Once again, this insight has multiple layers – physical, social, psychological and, at its depth – spiritual. You could spend a lifetime on this single teaching.

From the Heart ...

When you take away job, family reference and social context the consensual definition of self begins to dissolve. Carlos Castaneda called that "stopping the world." At first it is an odd feeling – this detaching from ordinary life. What is odd is that the references that you normally use to identity yourself are no longer in place. Whenever someone meets you, they immediately attempt to re-enforce the context. "What do you do?" is the common question. That is an attempt to define you by function. As you walk away from ordinary life, you become very aware of this definitional pressure. Inside, it feels like you are floating, without anchor. On the outside you feel increasingly like you don't belong; suspect even.

As time went on, I found it fun to make up stories as to what "I did for a living." I was a banker, a salesman, a merchant or administrator. It didn't matter, because what truly matters was defying inner defi-nitions of who I was. Only those who really knew me knew, and they had long since stopped the definitional games.

Some might look at this and say, "that's dishonest." Yes, it is. But everything in this world, particularly the definitions we form, are dishonest. And, my "playing" with this definitional situation had no negative side affects to those I "lied" to, because I would never let them closer than that definition. They wanted the definition, so I gave it to them. I became unashamed at disrobing like this. It was my way of "treading" on the "garment," as Jesus puts it in this insight.

The power of becoming unstuck to definitions is tremendous. You can move through social situations, varied contexts and gatherings without being locked into place. It gives the freedom needed to stay with the higher world of Spirit. I became the "trickster," like a coyote or a crow in Native American myth. This freedom helped me see, and the more I saw, the more I was able to avoid the traps. I became unafraid, because my knowledge of what was truly occurring was so much more than the social reality being played out. I begin to see "the living one," my True Self.

Insight 38

> *Jesus said, "Many times have you desired*
> *to hear these words which I am saying to you,*
> *and you have no one else to hear them from.*
> *There will be days when you will look*
> *for me and will not find me."*

From the Head ...

The Spirit is lost and forlorn in an alien world. In this insight, Jesus is directly addressing the Spirit. When read this way, it is very personal and loving, not a theological statement as most scholars usually assert. I think this insight should read like this: Jesus said, "I know how lonely and alien you feel, and there are so few who understand. Be strong! For there will be more days of loneliness, but also be assured, for your liberation has been achieved."

When translated this way, all of us can be touched by its depth and love. I imagine that when Jesus said these words, there were tears. Even writing them is powerful, from the perspective I suggest. When we search ourselves, we know the truth of this compassionate statement. We feel alone and lost. We long to be understood and helped along our way, but we also recognize how difficult life is, and that much of the work to be done has to be done within our solitary being. This is the truth of the Spirit's journey in this world.

This insight drives to the heart of our alienation and sense of lostness. As such, I count it among the truly loving sayings of Jesus, whose strength was not only his knowledge, but his great love and compassion.

From the Heart ...

I cannot read this insight without being moved. It feels so wonderful to be understood and truly seen as Spirit. Whenever we do that for one another, it is reassuring and liberating.

Along my path there have been a few truly enlightened beings who spoke with the heart of this insight. They knew what I felt without my having to say a word. They knew my loneliness and pain, without a single transaction. I miss them when they are not around, and yet somehow they are always with me.

The Spirit's journey here, so filled with pain and suffering, also becomes one of anticipation and joy. The knowledge that the spiritual connection is so great that the world of shadow cannot overcome it, is a great comfort when there are dark days. And be assured, there are dark days. We each weather those days in the way we can. There is no formula exactly, except the discipline of the Spirit that reminds you of the deeper truth to which you belong. There are few to talk to about this. Even fewer who will walk with you in this knowledge. But those who do, will be of the greatest joy to you, as they have been to me. When Jesus says, in his public sayings, "love one another," it is from this spiritual context that it must truly be understood.

Insight 39

> Jesus said, "The Pharisees and the scribes
> have taken the keys of knowledge (gnosis)
> and hidden them. They themselves have
> not entered, nor have they allowed to enter
> those who wish to. You, however, be as wise
> as serpents and as innocent as doves."

From the Head ...

To hide the keys of knowledge one must first have possession of them. That's what makes this warning so harsh. Jesus is saying that there are literally those who know the truth, and deliberately hide it from others, presumably to keep them under their rule and control.

The temptation to control with knowledge is great. This is basically the difference between sorcery and enlightenment. A sorcerer manipulates with his knowledge those things that are needed for his benefit. By this definition most everyone is a sorcerer. The question is whether they are good at it or bad, and to what degree their intentions are good or evil. A true sorcerer knows what he is practicing. Those who practice sorcery without knowing what they are doing are simply manipulators and users. In this insight, Jesus is saying that most religious leaders are sorcerers (he calls them Pharisees and scribes, but I take those labels to be rather generic and general, although he probably meant specifically those groups as well). Their goal is physical and emotional control, not liberation. How does Jesus know this? Because they themselves are not free and remain within the manipulative circle of the powers of this world. He warns his disciples however, that they know what they are doing. They have chosen a path, and their path is dark and hurtful.

This conflict between enlightened spirituality and sorcery is ongoing. Most spiritual practice today is sorcery – an attempt to manipulate the physical forces for some pre-determined goal or benefit of the small self that is existing in the world. Abundance theology and many healing techniques are sorcery in disguise. Some know the spiritual higher truth and simply chose to ignore it so they can use their power over people, and others are just ignorant fools going about a business they think is good, when in fact it has a manipulative edge to it.

Be aware, and beware. That is Jesus' advice. He further admonishes us to be careful with knowledge, since it is easy to fall prey to the power of the world and become, as George Lucas' "Star Wars" says of Darth Vader, seduced to the dark side.

From the Heart ...

There are those who have great knowledge, but chose the darkness of the world for their abode. They act as if they are light, but they are really filled with darkness. I have met some of these people, and my conflict with them is always immediate. They tend to take refuge in religious organizations, or quasi-religious structures. They seem so genuine and sincere, but they are as manipulative as they can be. Their goal is control, power and the draining of energy. My insight into them is this: they have the knowledge of their Spirit, but they keep it locked up so their lower psyche can control their life. In ancient Gnostic thinking on the subject, they subscribed to the understanding that some people were literally without the spark of light in them, and had only psychic and physical attributes. This may be. What I know for sure is, that if some people have spiritual knowledge and chose to hide it from themselves and others, it is truly diabolical.

"Be as wise as serpents and innocent as doves" is the last sentence of this insight. Those are two very different creatures: serpents and doves. Within our make-up as beings, these two forces get mixed together – which is why we get so confused. To be strong and smart, and at the same time be mild and innocent is, to say the least, an interesting balance. However, the more your Spirit awakens and your psychic self allies with that awakening, the easier this balance becomes. I have found it important to keep myself aware of the choices I am making at all times. This keeps my psyche alert to the temptation of becoming a sorcerer instead of the enlightened being I wish to be.

Insight 40

Jesus said, "A grapevine has been planted outside of the Father & Mother, but being unsound, it will be pulled up by its roots and destroyed."

From the Head . . .

Traditional scholarship on this saying places it in the realm of apocalyptic discourse, which does not fit in this collection. As usual, ordinary explanations and traditional scholarship doesn't have a clue. While the image of a grapevine is quite typical in the ancient world, this insight has a particular spin that makes it unique.

The grapevine that Jesus is speaking of is the world. It was "created" outside of the fullness of the divine realm (Father & Mother), and thus is unsound and has no real rooting in the everlasting. In Gnostic thinking on the subject, the material world is viewed as evil – not because it is immoral or disobedient, but because it is an inappropriate narrowing of reality into a hardened form. It therefore lacks the essential characteristics of the divine world. Evil, in this view, is the obsessive narrowing of reality that traps consciousness inside of its narrowed perceptive circle. That does not mean, of course, that the world does not have beauty or wonderful qualities. You cannot overlay traditional thinking on this subject, since evil is understood from a different perspective altogether.

When Jesus says that the world will be "pulled up by its roots and destroyed," he is saying that the essential lack within its narrowed reality scope is the flaw that will, eventually, destroy it. This is not apocalyptic in the usual sense – that some outside force will intervene to correct wrongs. This understanding is just an observation: that the world's process will die because it has death as its underpinning. Its death will be like an uprooting of a weed in the divine fullness, so it is not to be feared or thought of as tragic. The tragedy has already occurred in the obsessive narrowing of reality that is the world.

The grapevine (material world) is much like depression that can overcome an individual. It springs forth in the psyche and begins to rule over it. It takes on a life of its own. Its narrow reality traps consciousness inside of it's dark world, and becomes reality for the individual. Therapeutically, the idea is to break the hold of the narrowed reality and let the larger fullness of the psyche become reality.

This is what Jesus is driving at, although there are no first century words to express it other than this metaphor. This insight comes from Jesus' knowledge of who he is and where he now walks. As for all of us, the knowledge of who we really are is foundational to under-standing what is happening all around us. Our sense of alienation and loneliness tells us a great truth: we live in a "grapevine outside the Father and Mother" and that is exactly how it feels. However, that "Father and Mother" of the larger reality resides inside of us if we just allow it to come into our soul and speak to us. That which speaks to us from the divine realm apart from the narrowed reality of the world, is called gnosis (spiritual knowledge, or acquaintance). This gnosis is central to all of Jesus' insights.

From the Heart ...

This was a most difficult reality for me to grasp. Although I had always felt alienated and alone in the world, I was never taught nor told that it was the world that generated those feelings. Under all the religious perspectives and philosophies I studied was a sense of blame for feeling this way. In traditional Christianity, this alienation is caused by "sin," or "disobedience from the will of God." To overcome this sin Jesus had died on the cross, and my belief in that saving event would make my life whole and dissolve the alienation. I spent a great deal of my life believing that, or trying to believe it. But the alienation never went away.

Finally, I realized that alienation was not a characteristic that was developed psychologically, but was an existential truth of being that revealed itself psychologically. No matter what I believed about the world, or how many "good" decisions I made, I would still feel alienated. That truth would not go away, and when I read these insights, all my intuitions on the subject were validated.

Most of my spiritual quest was an attempt to eradicate this underlying sense of alienation. Oddly, when I finally understood the source of this alienation, it wasn't as extreme or difficult anymore. Not that it went away, but the alienation no longer had the ally of self-blame to augment it. All my spiritual work now began to pay off, since I was released from this terrible crime of "sin" against God. The world was "up-rooted" in me. Now I could stand outside of that alienation and aloneness and work with it. It became the first real step into a larger reality.

Insight 41

> Jesus said, "Whoever has something in his hand
> will receive more, and whoever has nothing
> will be deprived of even the little he has."

From the Head ...

This insight, like so many in this collection, is about our relationship to the world. Here the world is "nothing," and those who possess nothing literally have nothing. But even worse, their possession of "nothing" leads to severe despair and emptiness, so in essence, they are "deprived of even the little (they have)."

In traditional religious understanding, as is also seen in the general culture created by that religion, the world is going to transform into something wonderful and new. Whether this will be brought through the efforts of the community, or by God himself, something is expected to happen within the world to make it better and more meaningful. Jesus' position is contrary to that kind of expectation.

The world is "nothing" and can and will never be anything other than its nothingness. Efforts to change the fundamental meaninglessness and structure of the world process are all vanities of a false spirituality. Those who embrace the idea of a transforming historical process will be driven into utter disappointment and despair.

This point is affirmed in common language often. We say, "the more things change, the more they stay the same." That is exactly what Jesus is meaning here. You cannot alter the fundamental nature of something. As the old joke goes, "you can't teach a pig to sing – it costs a lot of money, and makes the pig mad."

Consequently, on the positive side of this statement, is the understanding that the larger spiritual reality will prevail, because its nature is everlasting and eternal. Many of Jesus' insights which seem negative and harsh have a powerful and positive backdrop from which he speaks. He drives home the necessity of seeing the truth about our situation because it is so easy to get lost in it – which it why he oft times emphasizes the negative. But they are always remarkably positive when seen from the vantage point of the Spirit.

From the Heart ...

In the last few years of my church ministry, I repeatedly made people angry because I talked about all this "negative" stuff. They wanted to come to church and feel good. They would say things like, "I come to church to feel better, not worse," or "Can't you just stop talking about all this negative stuff?" I became clear that most people were uncomfortable dealing with the existential reality of the world, and therefore could never really get what they truly needed – a deeper spiritual reality. They were locked into their "cotton candy" approach, and this generated a false sense of the spiritual – something that was fluffy and pretty, but had no substance. Those who engaged in an authentic search found that my "negative" teachings were very positive, and took great encouragement from them.

Essentially, I think this insight is very real and practical. Those who hold on to the world of "nothing" receive only empty verbiage and platitudes. Those who are willing to really see are given insights into the nature of truth itself. Their willingness is the "something" that helps them receive more.

I found that all those "hard" and difficult things in my spiritual journey were really the mines from which gold was to be discovered. As long as I mined at the easy stuff, I'd get nothing – just weak, tired answers. What Nietzsche suggested is true: "That which does not kill me makes me stronger." In my case it would read: that which is negative and difficult gives me insight.

Insight 42

Jesus said, "Become passers-by."

From the Head ...

This is the shortest of Jesus' teachings, but perhaps the most beautiful. It sums up Jesus' approach to spirituality. To become a "passer-by," one must not hold on to anything in this world. To hold on is to be stopped, and that is spiritual "death," for this world is not worthy of the Spirit.

This insight also advocates a certain lifestyle. It suggest that one should not place emphasis on places and things, and that life needs to be lived rather inaccessibly. To be inaccessible to the world means, as the Apostle Paul put it, "do not conform." To be a non-conformist is to practice non-attachment to the ordinary patterns of life. This may lead one to be a wanderer or homeless itinerant, or it may simply be an attitude within one's life. One can be a "passer-by" in many ways.

This insight had particular significance to Jesus' followers. Their lives were disrupted by this spiritual presence that was calling them to even deeper disruption. It was validating to hear Jesus speak of this truth. It's never easy to leave behind what they were called to leave behind. That is true for each of us. We are all bogged down much more than we think.

Also, this insight has internal significance as well. We have a tendency to attach to our feelings and thoughts about people, places and things. When we attach to particular features within ourselves, we are not free to let something live without our definition. This is a major difficulty in doing spiritual work. To become detached from worldly definitions is of critical importance. To be enlightened people, that is the very first thing that must be given in response to each and every person that is encountered: the freedom to be other than the definition the world has prescribed for them.

"Become passers-by." In this simple statement Jesus brings forth a great deal of reflection and thought. It has a depth within its simplicity, and a simplicity within its depth. It is at the heart of this collection.

From the Heart ...

This insight has been very meaningful for me. I have used it as a mantra in my spiritual life. Its power fills me, and then empties me. When I use its truth, I am lighter. When I don't, I am heavy.

Sometime back I wrote a prayer for myself using this insight. I print it here, because it is from my heart.

Prayer of the Passersby

O Divine Light that is my True
Father and Mother,
cradle my essence into your being.
Guide me to know my Divine origin,
and keep me safe within that knowledge.

Divine presence,
help me to hold no attachments
to the world of shadows
in which I find myself.
Develop in me a spiritual strength
that transcends all falsehood.

Lead me across the bridge of this world
and ignite in me the courage
to be a passerby.

Keep knowledge of your truth
a constant presence in my life.
And, keep my heart pure and
my mind keen to your whisper.

This life is a bridge –
I shall walk over it.
I shall visit many things,
but find only a home in you,
O Divine Light.

May my Spirit soar
to the Light,
and may my heart rejoice
in the knowledge of the truth.
Amen.

Insight 43

*His disciples said to him, "Who are you, that you
should say these things to us?" Jesus said to them
"You do not realize who I am from what I say to you,
but you have become like the Jews, for they
(either) love the tree and hate its fruit
(or) love the fruit and hate the tree."*

From the Head ...

It's amazing how we accept half-truths and cut ourselves off from
the larger sense of knowledge that is needed for authentic spirituality.
This insight is about that problem. "The Jews," which is a metaphor
for all religions, tends to only reveal truth that justifies the institutional
structure of the organization. This insight ["love the tree and hate its
fruit, (or) love the fruit and hate the tree"] is a beautiful way to make
this point. It teaches the difference between whole and half truths.

To love the tree and the fruit is a spiritually mature position, since
the fruit cannot be without the tree, and the tree has so many
purposes other than the fruit that is enjoyed. The fruit of the Tree of
Knowledge is gnosis, and the Tree is the spiritual realm itself. To have
eaten from the Tree is to have tasted the reality of the Tree. In religion
it is a temptation to eat from the fruit of the Tree and not allow the
larger reality to give shade and coolness from the dust and heat of the
world. Jesus complains that this problem with religion blocks people
from seeing and literally gets them diverted onto a hurtful and wrong
path. This insight, and those like it, are meant to keep us aware and
attuned to what we are seeing and focusing on.

Another important aspect of this saying comes at the beginning:
"Who are you, that you should say these things to us?" It is always

difficult to get beyond our definitions of people. Jesus was a carpenter from Galilee. That which spoke through him was the divine Spirit, which we designate with the title "Christ." The disciples understood that something was happening inside of Jesus that was not Jesus' ordinary self. To ask: "Who are you?" is not an angry question as it might sound here, but a genuine one coming from a puzzled group of followers not knowing what they are experiencing. The metaphor of the Tree and its Fruit is the best way of telling the disciples that he is speaking from the realm that is both.

From the Heart ...

In the last few months of my traditional ministry I found myself teaching in ways that I couldn't explain the source. It was like a force of wisdom had "walked into" me. It wasn't that I felt differently or even acted differently, but when it came time for me to teach, it was like something literally came over me. I became aware that this presence was an opening to something that had its being in another realm. In private I would ask "Who are you?" It never spoke to me like a voice. It was just a presence. Was I "channeling" something? Or, was this presence the awakened Spirit within me now coming to the forefront? It was the latter, of course. But this awakened Spirit was an alien presence nevertheless. Alien in the sense of being strange and different from the world.

People commented on a perceptual change in my countenance as I taught. I'd laugh about it with them, as we had no explanation other than the limited ones I had groped to find. I've come to be more comfortable with it now, wanting to have access to that presence on a more regular basis. That presence is the authentic "I" of my True Self, and gets "channeled" (I hate to use that word, because it is so overused and poorly understood by New Age quasi-religionists, but it's the best word I can come up with) into my mind and feelings.

This insight helps me understand what is happening with myself. The Tree is connecting with the Fruit, and when that occurs, my True Self has access to my conscious life. Those who are having this experience confirm to me the reality and truth of my own sense of it. It is very powerful. It also connects you to others who are having this experience as well. It is like you just know.

Insight 44

> Jesus said, "Whoever blasphemes against the father will be forgiven, and whoever blasphemes against the son will be forgiven, but whoever blasphemes against the holy spirit will not be forgiven either on earth or in heaven."

From the Head ...

This insight contains the formulation Father, Son and Holy Spirit – which is an idea of the later church. Most likely, therefore, it is an insertion. However, I think there is value in this saying, even though on the surface of it, it seems a bit harsh and "un-Jesus" like.

The idea of the Holy Spirit is important in that it refers to the feminine principle within the divine. This feminine principle is the nurturing, loving and caring component. Unfortunately in the early church, as with many theological constructions of those years, the feminine side of God was all but ignored. This saying is an attempt to bring focus and balance to the idea of the divine. You cannot deny the nurturing, sensitive side of the divine and have that principle work in your life. To ignore forgiveness is to evade the power of forgiveness. If God is loving, then God has this wonderful feminine side. The divine is whole, not part.

At first reading this insight appears to be judgmental, but like so many of these insights, it has a quality that transcends the language. The idea of the divine as "Father and Son" is ancient, but what's missing? Mother, of course (sister, too, for that matter!). The Holy Spirit is the balancing factor in that formulation. In later Gnostic expression there is more direct reference to the Father and Mother of light, but here is it cloaked in the idea of Holy Spirit.

Another important point to be made here is that the Spirit lost in the material world, which is central to the theme of all these insights, are aspects of a feminine emanation from the divine realm. What that means is this: the Spirit within is feminine. So, in denying the Holy Spirit, one denies one's True Self. Ultimately, this insight is not about "forgiveness" on the level that we usually think of it, but on the larger level of self-knowledge. Forgiveness becomes a metaphor for self-awareness and knowledge (gnosis). Without self-awareness and gnosis, a true sense of self cannot be achieved. One cannot know one's self without awareness of that knowledge. That is the primary point of this insight.

From the Heart ...

We are trained to think of the divine in certain ways that control and manipulate us. Formulating God as Father and Son without reference to the feminine is an outright manipulation intended to scare us. Without really being aware of it, I was always emotionally afraid of God. Who wouldn't be? After all, God had his only son sacrificed – guess what he'll do to you? God is so angry in the orthodox and traditional Bible that one cannot avoid being emotionally intimated by all that power that seems to be angry. Jesus, in that formulation, is a great deal kinder, but he's a victim of a cosmic drama being played out, and for the most part, people feel guilty about his sacrifice anyway. Which is why, I suppose, a cult of Mary has been generated in the Catholic Church. It's a way to avoid the cruelty and victimization within orthodox thinking.

Intellectually I had moved beyond all this many years ago, but it wasn't until I did a great deal of inner work that I discovered that the emotional fear was still there. There is only one way of resolving that fear: self-knowledge. When you become aware that your True Self is beyond the scope of all the petty tyranny being played out in this cosmic drama, you begin to have a sense of release. Self-knowledge is critical. Without that knowledge no amount of prayer, intellectual-ization or pleading will help. My realization that the self in me was greater than all of the created and organized world of form and shadow, was the first step into what this insight suggests. With self-knowledge we stop "blaspheming" against the Holy Spirit – which ultimately comes down to being the spark that is within us.

Insight 45

> Jesus said, "Grapes are not harvested from thorns,
> nor are figs gathered from thistles, for they do not produce
> fruit. A good man brings forth good from his storehouse; an
> evil man brings forth evil things from his evil storehouse
> which is in his heart, and says evil things. For out of the
> abundance of the heart he brings forth evil things."

From the Head . . .

It's important to remember that evil, in the sense that it is used in these insights, is not understood in the usual way. Evil is the narrowing of reality. It is basically denial of the larger whole in favor of a small constructed reality that gets born out of the whole. The world itself is evil, in that it is a small "created" reality that denies the larger divine realm. We participate in evil when we focus, wittingly or unwittingly, on that reality as the only reality.

Again in this insight, the world is seen as "thorns" and "thistles." It cannot produce "fruit," since it denies anything other than its own created myopic reality set. Like a depressed person who is locked within his depression, the world is dark and hurtful. The depressed person is not aware that there is a larger consciousness behind the depression, and therefore the depression becomes reality. That is what Jesus is asserting here about the world.

To understand this insight, moralistic thinking must be placed aside. Jesus is dealing on a level that most of us have denied in our reality. That, of course, is the evil in our hearts. But the "heart" contains so much more than the reality that we commonly focus on.

A person of gnosis brings forth the larger reality ("a good man brings forth good from his storehouse"), and sees the truth of it.

The small narrow reality of the world "pressures" the Spirit into sleep and intoxication, and traps its essence in the narrow focus of its process. To break out of that "pressure," the larger reality must break through and grab hold of the lost part of consciousness that it trapped there, and pull it out. It is slippery business – filled with "thorns" and "thistles" (forces of psychological and biological pressure).

This insight cuts to the issue. Narrowed reality sustains itself by producing a self validating narrow view. It is a circle feeding on itself, like the urouboros (snake biting its own tail) of old. Evil produces evil, good produces good. Evil equals the false narrowed reality, good equals the authentic larger whole.

From the Heart ...

The world in which we live is like an onion, with layers upon layers. I envision us living at the core of that onion, surrounded by these layers that we don't even see. As we begin the process of peeling away the layers reaching ever outward, our reality vision expands, until all the layers are gone, and our vision is not blocked by any of the onion's layers. What lies beyond the onion? The fullness, or vastness. In the fullness are many such small realities, as within each of us are many galaxies and constellations of emotions, thoughts, beliefs and personality features. I am all of this, and not just this small thing wandering around in some earthly body.

Much of my life was spent in one layer of the onion. That's where most of us spend our time. We never see that beyond that layer are other layers. Of interest to me is how captivating these layers are. Even as you escape one for another, you can get fascinated with the outer layer. It's no more a full reality than the one you just escaped, but its difference stops you from your journey. I know many people who became so fascinated with moving between the layers of reality that they were just as caught as before without realizing it. Many shamanic leaders are trapped in this movement between the layers – so fascinated that they re-invest themselves with the intoxication they sought to leave behind.

It's easy to get lost within the smallness! To remain fluid, and not become enamored of the movement between the realities is an act of gnosis, for each and every layer of the onion is a trap. Like with a bush of thorns and thistles, it's so easy to get tangled up.

Insight 46

> Jesus said, "Among those born of women,
> from Adam until John the Baptist, there is no one
> superior to John the Baptist that his eyes should not be
> lowered (before him). Yet I have said, whichever one of
> you comes to be a child will be acquainted with the
> kingdom and will become superior to John."

From the Head ...

Think of the greatest person that you can. Who would it be? Thomas Jefferson? Jesus? The Buddha? Albert Einstein? Whoever that person is, or was, Jesus is teaching here, is less significant than the Spirit that is in you. This insight illustrates how important finding one's True Self is. All human endeavor and personages are nothing in comparison to the glory of the Spirit. All personalities and individuals in this life are but shadows of that which lies beyond it in the spiritual realm.

It is clear from this insight that the followers of Jesus were very impressed with John the Baptist. He was viewed as a great man. But Jesus is pointing them inward to that which rests inside of them, teaching that acquaintance with the True Self is superior to even the most revered person they can think of.

This insight was perhaps shocking to the disciples. It would be like a devoted Christian being told that inside of them was something more significant than the human person of Jesus, who Christians have come to worship and revere. "Comes to be a child" refers to the gnosis of the authentic True Self of the Spirit; being a child of the divine, or spark of the divine realm. Here, in this insight, Jesus is reinforcing what he has taught many times ("Yet I have said ... "), because it is central to all his teachings.

From the Heart ...

It is our great temptation to make someone an idol or god. When we do, we detach from the divinity within ourselves, and lose the essence of who *we* truly are. While it is appropriate to revere and respect those who lead the way, they themselves have no more than we do, when we see the truth of the Spirit.

Another aspect of this is the difference between having faith in something, and knowing something. Having faith is trusting in someone else's knowledge, while having knowledge is trusting your own experience. Years ago, when I was a student, I literally worshipped those who I felt had such great knowledge and insight. As I became more aware, and found deep truth for myself, I maintained respect for those I had learned from, but I no longer held them up in godlike awe.

The primary problem in orthodox Christianity is that it makes this same mistake. People worship Jesus as the Christ, and yet they never become the Christ that they in fact truly are. This objectification is a narrowing of reality, that in Gnostic thinking is evil (idolatry in the usual language). It is a looking away from the truth, rather than looking toward the truth.

In the traditional public Gospel of John, Jesus is said to have said: "I am the way, the truth and the life. No one comes to the father except by me." I can believe that Jesus said that, because each one of us could say that. We each are the way and the truth. No one comes to the father and mother of light except by way of their Spirit. As I grew in understanding, sayings like this became quite commonplace and routine. They were obvious.

Insight 47

> Jesus said, "It is impossible for a man to mount
> two horses or to stretch two bows. And it is impossible
> for a servant to serve two masters; otherwise he will honor
> the one and treat the other contemptuously. No man
> drinks old wine and immediately desires to drink new
> wine. And new wine is not put into old wineskins, lest
> they burst; nor is old wine put into a new wineskin,
> lest it spoil it. An old patch is not sewn into a
> new garment, because a tear would result."

From the Head ...

This insight, like those in the public Gospels that resemble it, is meant to focus us and bring our attention into clarity. Every saying here is a time honored one. Jesus probably did not invent any of these sayings – they were common lore. But Jesus is using them in a special way. He is teaching: a person of knowledge cannot acknowledge their True Self by denying their True Self.

What difference does spirituality make? What happens to the person who comes to knowledge (gnosis)? This insight suggests that the change is total in a person's loyalty and allegiance. What was important to a person becomes unimportant or even repugnant after knowledge of the True Self is acquired. Friends and associations change, and a person of knowledge begins a life of solitary understanding, meaning that the world's knowledge no longer matters.

These sayings are like an old Iroquois saying: "A man who has a foot in two canoes soon falls in the water." So, Jesus is making the most out of common lore that can be helpful in instructing people about the spiritual journey, and the radical nature of its requirement. This kind of insightful teaching is what made Jesus so brilliant at being the guide he was.

From the Heart ...

As I came to trust the gnosis with all my heart, my life changed. It was not possible for me to keep going in the workaday world with all its concessions to truth and all of its illusory promises. The world seemed far less appealing. To seek the freedom of the Spirit became the only real purpose – for the Spirit was the only authentic reality.

I find it difficult to stand in two worlds. Exactly what this insight suggests is true: you begin to hate one and honor the other, but in the hating of the lesser reality you lose something of yourself. Too much energy is involved with hatred. It takes away from the soul's vision of the Spirit.

In early Gnostic thinking, a solitary life was encouraged. Solitary in the sense that one was encouraged to seek his own inner knowledge and advice, but also to store away a private life of the Spirit. I don't think this necessarily meant that you had to keep away from all things in the world, but to keep focus away from those attachments, illusions and false realities that drive us into spiritual sleep.

For me, it has become increasingly impossible to put "new wine into old wine skins" – putting my spiritual self into the ordinariness of the world. I am careful as to how I focus, and what I intend. The seduction of the world system is so great that I feel that I cannot afford to be taken off guard.

Insight 48

Jesus said, "If two make peace with each other in this one house, they will say to the mountain, 'Move away,' and it will move away."

From the Head ...

On the surface this saying appears as if it has an external meaning: that agreement alters the material matrix of reality itself. A mountain can be moved by people making peace with each other. Liberal theologians often interpret this as a kind of "social gospel" saying, which implies that people can change the world if we make peace with one another. And to be sure, some of this is meant. But its real meaning is interior.

The two that are to "make peace with each other" are the soul and the Spirit. The one house is the body, and the mountain is the world. When the soul and Spirit agree and work in accord, the world mountain dissolves as a power – it "move(s) away," as this insight suggests.

On the exterior side of this insight is the truth that "the mountain" (the world) is an obstacle to spiritual peace. To move it away from priority takes agreement within and without. Agreement becomes an aspect of gnosis. To agree with the true knowledge of the Spirit allows peace between individuals, as well as creating inner tranquillity.

From the Heart ...

The warfare between soul and Spirit goes unnoticed until that warfare cannot be avoided. The soul – locked into a focus that the world gives it as a motivation and drive – cannot see the nature of the Spirit, nor its reality until that reality is revealed to it. The tension can be incredible.

The truth of a reality beyond this world was a conflict of the highest order to my soul. I found it difficult to accept that something in me was higher than my mental, emotional and thinking attributes (which are all aspects of the soul). What "controlled" me was my psychological self, and the Spirit was a threat to that control mechanism. This was a kind of inner warfare that I began to see played out in everything I did, believed and felt. I was more attached to the world than I had ever conceived, especially since the idea of non-attachment had never occurred to me at all.

The conflict between my Spirit and my soul and body became intense, as it remains to this day. Peace was made when my soul and body yielded to the truth of my higher self, or as it is often referred to as: "the True Self." This yielding required me to put away the things that forced me to act as I had in the past. Insecurity, loneliness, intense sexual desire, the need to "fit in" – all these things were aspects of my lower self which controlled my self-identity, that now yielded to the alien quality above all these issues.

The most fundamental "agreement" that was made in my life was internal; a time when all parts of me converged into the truth of who I really was. I felt the mountain move, as this insight suggests, which meant that I was no longer a part of the mountain itself – it was "away" from me.

Insight 49

> Jesus said, "Blessed are the solitary and elect,
> for you will find the Kingdom. For you are
> from it, and to it you will return."

From the Head . . .

"For you are from it, and to it you will return." This theme is central to all of Jesus' sayings. This saying, and the next, focus specifically on the alien origin of the Spirit, and the return of that Spirit to its own reality. Listen to this insight as a deep wonderment, a truth longed for, and you will know what the disciples felt when they heard it.

In our modern world we have been brainwashed into thinking of ourselves as merely physically evolved creatures, that such a saying seems indeed alien and from another world. We are comprised of such complexities – in part evolved from the matrix of the world, and partly from something beyond. This mixture confuses and obscures true knowledge. Like many of these sayings, it confirms what we already suspect about ourselves: that part of us doesn't belong here in this world. We feel and sense our alienation, and generally we pass it off as some difficulty in our thinking or emotions. The truth is that our alienation comes from something far deeper, and has a more positive meaning. We feel alienated because our Spirit is alien. When you are alone, you feel the power of this. It selects (elects!) you from that solitary position, where it cannot be avoided. It is the kingdom of the divine realm – the Spirit world.

This saying also encourages us to spend time alone with ourselves. We become so involved in the relational and social world that we have created and is created for us, that we forget who we really are, and sleep to the deepest part of ourselves. The "kingdom" is not found in a church, or in an organization of any kind. It is discovered inside. How can one discover that which is inside when it is not valued and honored? Jesus, once again, points his friends inward to find the truth for themselves.

From the Heart ...

Twenty-five years ago when I first read this saying in a sourcebook in a church history class in seminary, it moved me to tears. At the time, I passed it off as silly – something was "bothering me." I avoided thinking about how this saying, and others like it, affected me. I put this material down, and didn't look at it again for decades. When I read it years later, I had the same response. It touched me at some level that I could not explain, and confirmed something that I had always felt – my "alien-ness."

It wasn't until I pulled away into aloneness and solitariness that this insight reached its full impact. I had "fallen" into the world – and somewhere I had known that, but forgotten it, or "slept" to it. This insight literally awakened something in me – like a familiar voice calling to me in a strange and alien land. The more I listened, the more it rang true, and called me deeper into the mystery of my True Self.

It is of interest to me now, that for some years I walked around with this inner mystery unfolding, and yet spoke not a word of it. It took along time for it to "gel" into place in my soul. Finally, the link between my soul and Spirit became the guiding fact in my earthly life. I then knew what it meant to be "solitary" and "elect." At first it seemed a curse, because it divided me from everything I had valued and believed in. But then! It became the blessing, for I could see what I had lost and now found – and that was the great marvel and wonder.

Insight 50

> Jesus said, "If they say to you, 'Where did you
> come from?', say to them, 'We came from the light,
> the place where the light came into being on its own
> accord and established itself and became manifest
> through their image.' If they say to you, 'Is it you?' say,
> 'We are its children, and we are the elect of the living
> father and mother. If they ask you, 'What is the
> sign of your father in you?', say to them,
> 'It is movement and repose.' "

From the Head ...

This saying, like the one previous to it, speaks directly about the central insight that Jesus shares with people: awakening to an inner truth of self. In their awakening people are always concerned with what to say about it, to others and to themselves. This insight helps put into words what is felt in the heart. To say "I came from the light and I am a child of that light" is a radical statement. What it means is that the Spirit is uncreated and existed before the world was. Not made of mud and clay, like the Old Testament says of the created form of ourselves, the Spirit is divine in origin. It came from the light itself where that light "establishes itself."

"What is the sign ... in you?" The Spirit itself, the "movement and repose." The world is lost in its own dynamics and movement – fascinated by its own suffering and darkness. But the Spirit remains in peace, untouched by the darkness. It sleeps to its reality until awakened, and upon awakening, knows itself and its true home. This is a simple expression of all of Jesus' teachings; his central theme.

While many scholars look at this saying as "far removed" from the language and ideas of Jesus (*The Five Gospels*, "The Jesus Seminar" – Robert Funk and Roy Hoover, p. 502), they seem to not notice that their perception is dictated by incestuous thinking, namely, that the public Gospels are used to validate themselves. A kind of circular logic that scholars have fallen prey to since the beginning of the debate over the "historical Jesus." I think the larger truth is, that Jesus was far more radical than they suppose, and this insight is suggestive of that radical character that ignited and irritated the people of his time. For imagine what it would mean for someone to come to an understanding that inside of them is something so great that the world cannot and will never understand it. It would, indeed, set you apart from the ordinary world of ideas and social convention – which is what Jesus preached and did.

From the Heart ...

Once you begin discovering the truth of these insights, everything changes – as I have suggested before. You walk through the world differently. I can't explain it exactly, but it is noticeable, and people are bothered by it. They begin to ask you about it, sometimes supposing that something is wrong with you. They tend to take your detached approach to life as depression or avoidance of something – neither of which it is. For me, all this insight is attempting to do is to make one aware of that which is the obvious result of spiritual awakening. But I also discovered something more to this teaching: it has a kind of metaphysical power to it.

This teaching, like so many, has a dual purpose – the obvious and the hidden. The hidden agenda here is to instruct one to speak to the "powers" and "rulers" of this world system words that will subdue and overcome them. I have discovered that it works! For those who are unclear as to whether there are forces mindfully working to keep us trapped in this system, this will sound strange and odd, but maintaining true identity as a being from the Spirit world is essential to avoiding the pitfall of falling prey to the cycle of life. This cycle of life, which is really a trap meant to enslave the Spirit as a "food" source for the system, seeks to keep us locked into place. These simple words of Jesus literally free you from that bondage, since it names you as a being from outside its territory.

This revelation cannot be seen from the outside in, like one would study something scientifically. It is a "mystery" that is seen only from the eyes of the Spirit itself. Now, as circular as that sounds, it occurs that way. As I saw from my Spirit eyes, what Carlos Castaneda called "seeing," I could see the truth of this insight. I needed to maintain my identity, or I would be lost again. That became no speculative thought for me, but a practical guide.

Insight 51

*His disciples said to him,
"When will the repose of the dead come about
and when will the new world come?" He said to them,
"What you look forward to has already come,
but you do not recognize it."*

From the Head ...

We tend to view things materially. Even when we talk about the Spirit, we use language that evokes physical images, and so it is no surprise that people often get caught up in looking for some thing to happen. This has been the mistake of orthodox religions from the beginning, and it is a darkness from which we must recover if we are to truly see.

Jesus is saying that the world as it is will never change, but what we desire is already here, and has always been – before the world was. We just do not know how to see, or that we need to see. Spiritual sleep fills our eyes.

To their credit, the disciples here understood that "the dead" are all those living in the world. This world is the place of the dead. It is the hell we fear will come after we die. But true life, the Spirit world, is here also, and yet it cannot be recognized from the eyes of the world. This insight brings our focus back inside again. To see our True Self is to see the new world. That is Jesus' point. He makes it over and over again. The key to staying awake is reminding oneself of the Spirit world often. Jesus practices this with his disciples, and uses their questions as opportunities for awakening.

From the Heart ...

Nietzsche wrote: "Man is a rope stretched between the animal and the Superman – a rope over the abyss" (*Thus Spake Zarathustra*, "Zarathustra's Prologue," p. 8). This saying feels to me much like Jesus' insights. The idea is that man himself is the bridge between worlds, that what we long for is within us already if we could just see it.

As I reflect I see that before awakening, my life was about goals and objectives to be met. I set goals to achieve, achieved them, and identified myself by that achievement. I became my function and my "doing" in the world. To awaken to something beyond all of the goals, aspirations and achievements was to awaken to what Nietzsche called the "Superman." In my awakening I felt as if I had overcome something that was dragging me down. I felt release from the shame and guilt of my being (as Nietzsche often preached!), and could feel myself "stretched" over the world as a bridge.

There is an old saying: "Life is a bridge, cross over it." I'm unsure as to whether its origin is Buddhist or Gnostic, but it doesn't matter. It rings true. To "cross over " the world one must first cross over the notions of self contrived by the world, and become free to move with inner peace (repose) to the authentic self of the Spirit.

To remind myself of my True Self, I would often leave notes posted in places that I would see which would cause me to remember. On the mirror in the bathroom, in my car, or books I was reading – I would stick a saying or special reference. Any place that I would happen across, I wanted to remind myself of who I was, so that the world would not take that knowledge from me again. Now, I find, I have less and less need of those artificial reminders. My soul knows! I remind myself.

Insight 52

*His disciples said to him, "Twenty-four prophets spoke in
Israel, and all of them spoke in you." He said to them,
"You omitted the one living in your presence
and have spoken only of the dead."*

From the Head ...

Sometimes we miss something important that is right in front of
us. Here we have spiritually minded people doing that. We tend to
make tradition and history normative, and judge from that basis. This
is what religion is all about. The prophets, or Holy literature of
Judaism, which is referred to here as the "Twenty-four prophets,"
had become the normative basis of Judaism and revered religiously.
Jesus is simply asking the disciples to see what is happening *now*, and
stop looking at what was.

From a practical point of view, closing a body of Holy literature in
an attempt to capture the essence of the religious notion, has been the
norm in religion. A Holy Book is then formed, and generally
speaking, that book becomes the centerpiece of the religion. But in
truth, this practice is a darkness, for while practical in forming a
normative basis of judgment, it also stops the fluidity and drama of
the Spirit. People become fixated on the literature instead of the experience. Everything begins to revolve around "The Book," as a criteria
as to whether something is "of the religion" or not.

Perhaps what Jesus is driving at here is that no literature or religion
can capture the reality and drama of the Spirit. When we allow
ourselves to think that it does, or has some kind of special significance, it becomes an avenue of darkness instead of enlightenment
precisely because we miss the movement in front of us. Where is our

focus? Where are we looking? The answers we seek are never written on a page, or contained in some body of literature. The best that any book or body of literature can do is point a way, not "The Way," but a way to something. The real action is always beyond language.

From the Heart ...

As a minister for 25 years, I was often asked: "Which Bible should I read?" This referred to the dilemma many people feel about all the choices in translations available of the Christian Bible. I shocked them usually by saying, "Take a year and live with your own spiritual reality before you read about others." Some would ask then, "How will I learn about Christianity then?" I would tell them, "Learning about Christianity is not the ultimate goal. Learning about the ways of the Spirit is." "Christianity," I would continue, "is a body of literature about the spiritual essence that moves in and around us. It is not that movement itself." I suppose I was a heretic from the beginning.

I've come to be rather anti-religious. I mean that in the sense that religion is more of a problem than it is a solution to the spiritual bankruptcy that is felt by most people today. Church is about church – not enlightenment. That was a hard reality for me to learn, but learn it I did, over and over again. I didn't want to live my life in that fashion, or within that darkness.

For me, the greatest spiritual stuff happens in front of us beyond all the intellectual language. It happens in our experience of the spiritual reality that leads us into that "separate reality" that cannot be explained with all our books and words. Yes, books are valuable and important, but only to a limited degree. After that, one has to seek inside himself what the Spirit says. As that truth sank in to me, the more I pulled away from conventional religion, into a solitary path – which I found was shared, ironically, by many people. That new way became my "religion."

Insight 53

*His disciples said to him, "Is circumcision
beneficial or not?" He said to them, "If it were beneficial,
their father would beget them already circumcised from
their mother. Rather, the true circumcision in
spirit has become completely profitable."*

From the Head ...

Once again, this saying is a help to those struggling with overcoming the tradition of their religion. Circumcision was a hot issue
during this time. Whether someone was circumcised symbolized
their belonging to the religious sect or not. Jesus is making fun of the
idea by saying, "If it were beneficial, their father would beget them
already circumcised from their mother." I imagine everyone hearing
this laughed.

True circumcision, which is symbolic of belonging to the Spirit for
Jesus, comes in spiritual ways. It does not have outward manifesta-
tions that are easily recognizable. No religion contains it, and no any
symbol fully reflects it. That is the point being made here.

From the Heart ...

"Are you a Christian?" I am constantly being asked this question.
Sometimes, to just avoid a struggle over terminology, I'll say, "sure."
But Christianity has become an irrelevant issue to me. The question
isn't whether someone adheres to a certain set of beliefs, but whether
they know their true essence. The question should be: "Do you know
who you are?"

When I'm asked whether I'm a "Christian" I think of this insight from Jesus. I think, if being a Christian were important we'd all be born with little crosses around our necks. Who cares? That's the real point. Do we honestly think that God cares about our religion? Is that what God cares about – our doctrines and rituals of dogma? I don't think so.

The divine cares about finding itself. That is what is happening in the Spirit realm. The divine finds itself and rejoices, which is what makes discovery of our True Self so critical. That is all the doctrine I need. That is all the religion I want. Period.

don't even know they exist. They just raise their heads when we least expect it. That is where the hard work is done – the cross, as this insight puts it.

Insight 56

> Jesus said, "Whoever has come to understand
> the world has found only a corpse, and whoever
> has found a corpse is superior to the world."

From the Head ...

Valentinus, the second century Gnostic author of The Gospel of Truth, calls the world "an error." That the world with all its suffering, death and blind process should be termed "a corpse" or an "error" is very much in keeping with the idea of a spiritual reality beyond the world that is perfect. In this insight, Jesus is driving home the difference between the realities in which we find ourselves. The world is so deficient in meaning and process as to be termed a corpse, while the Spirit world is "superior to the world."

This depreciation of the world stands in stark contrast to the elevation of the world and the depreciation of man that is found in orthodox thinking. Jesus saw the world as a place of suffering and intoxication of the Spirit, much like the Buddha, whose first noble truth is: Life is suffering. For Jesus, that suffering is overcome through self-knowledge – the knowledge that one's True Self is ultimately beyond the reach and power of the material matrix. The Spirit is asleep to its true nature, and when awakened finds itself in an alien land filled with death and decay. It is hellish.

For Gnostics, the world came into being by accident, or a divine mistake. Its hardened reality creates an objectification of the Spirit that is inappropriate and not part of the divine wholeness. The Spirit must return to its original home in the divine wholeness to escape the terrible hell of the world. This escape is accomplished through knowledge (gnosis) of the Spirit – which is the true being that resides within the molded "clay" of the body. Everything other than the Spirit has illusory life, and will pass away. That is why it is called a corpse in this text. He who finds the world corpse is said to be superior, for in finding it, the Spirit understands itself to be beyond the limited essence of material life. This understanding, far from being a terrible horror, is a great joy. For in knowing the True Self, death is dissolved, and suffering is minimized as a mere function of something so inferior as to be ignored. Those who heard this insight found it very uplifting and joyous, for it affirms the immortal Spirit – not by faith, but by its mere essence. Whether one is granted eternal life because of faith or simply has eternal life by mere essence, is also part of this complex religious debate. For Jesus in these private sayings, spiritual knowledge is central and definitive for liberation, not faith in an external doctrine or dogmatic code.

It must be remembered that this saying, like the rest of these insights, are spoken to those whom Jesus held in close regard. He spoke bluntly to them, so as to instruct them in detail. Unlike speaking to the "masses," which the public Gospels do, Jesus in these texts takes his teachings to a deeper level, with harder comments. It should not surprise us that these sayings are unlike those of the public Gospels – not only because they intend different things and are spoken to different groups, but also because the public Gospels omit language that would have been difficult for those uninitiated into deeper understanding, and would have been counter-productive to the creation of an institutional church.

From the Heart . . .

Finding the world a corpse is ceasing to find it as ultimately meaningful. The world, both the human social and political construct, and the process of the natural order, hold nothing that has any real value or substance to it – other than the Spirit underneath that unwittingly gives it life. I know that sounds a bit harsh and strange, but it is true. What we learn to hold in such high esteem and honor, has no lasting essence at all. Ultimately, the world is nothing – it will die. The earth, the solar system, and the universe itself – all dead. A corpse. We know this, of course, but we exclude it from our conscious life. This is one way that the Spirit is kept asleep from its own reality.

The Spirit, on the other hand, does not die. It is not held to the standards of contrived reality and limited situational morality. Radical, yes. To say, as Jesus did, and all who understand themselves spiritually, that we are superior to the world, sounds elitist. And, it is I suppose, from one point of view. But, like Dizzy Dean once said, "It ain't braggin' if you can do it." It just is.

To be honest, I didn't have that much trouble with this insight. It sounded pretty accurate at first reading. Others, especially those who have confused beauty with meaningfulness and goodness, find this saying a bit harder to cope with. After all, they say, doesn't the world have some wonderful things in it? Doesn't life sometimes feel great? Doesn't it hold love and kindness sometimes, and hold vast wonders to behold? Of course! I have no doubts about that. But there is something wrong. The above arguments sound a lot like my ten year old son who claims nothing is better than macaroni and cheese. He refuses to taste anything outside of his small tastebuds. I, too, felt that way once, but then I got a taste of something more and greater, and now macaroni and cheese, while okay, isn't my idea of a great meal.

The Spirit world is so vast and wondrous as to make the hardened form of materiality like macaroni and cheese compared to a French Chef's fine creation. Valentinus called it "deficient," and that is precisely how it feels. If you stayed focused on physicality and social/political realities, your life becomes so bankrupt as to have no real meaning at all. Yes, that's a little preachy, but it's the truth for me. The world is a corpse. That's okay with me. I'm not part of that anyway. Neither are you.

Insight 57

> Jesus said, "The kingdom of the father and mother
> is like a man who had good seed. His enemy came by
> night and sowed weeds among the good seed. The man did
> not allow them to pull up the weeds; he said to them,
> 'I am afraid that you will go intending to pull up the weeds
> and pull up the wheat along with them.' For on the day
> of the harvest the weeds will be plainly visible,
> and they will be pulled up and burned."

From the Head ...

Alchemy in the middle ages was a "science" concerned with the extracting of gold from base metals. The basic idea was that gold could be found within all metals if the impurity was somehow dissolved. The idea that something valuable was mixed within the impure world was the basis of alchemy, and the basis of this insight. The issue is: how do you extract that which is pure and important, from that which is a mixed base? How does the Spirit become retrieved from the mix in which it is lost? This parable is a beautiful example of Jesus' insight into this situation.

Taken on the surface, this insight appears to have a judgmental flavor to it. There are those a are "weeds" and those who are "good seed." But it goes far beyond that. It drives to the heart of Jesus' teaching with regard to the mixture of the Spirit in the world. The "weeds" are the forces of the world that seek to strangle the Spirit, and keep it trapped in a slumbering bondage. One must be very careful, Jesus is stating. Things are very confusing in this world. Sometimes you think you are dealing with a weed, but in fact it is a spiritual reality. At other times, the opposite is true. It takes great discernment and ability to do the work of a spiritual alchemist.

The "day of the harvest" is every day, of course. The weeds will be "plainly visible" to those who know what they are looking for. The catch is, one has to know what one is seeing. Weeds and wheat can look very much like each other. To nurture a Spirit awake is, therefore, tricky business. Recall that St. Paul echoed this insight in saying: it is not flesh and blood that we struggle against, but powers and principalities. The mixture requires spiritual maturity and clarity of perception. Jesus' task here is to make clear the difficulty of the work to be done.

From the Heart ...

There were times when the voices in my head were very confusing. I wasn't sure whether I was listening to some psychological issue filtered through my intellect, or a pure Spirit that gave me knowledge and truth. How was I to know the difference? What alchemy could I use – what magic was available? The answer was very simple, so simple I would have ignored it if it weren't so clear. Patience. The Spirit outlasts the issues. An "issue" will bounce all over the place, but the Spirit will remain at peace with itself. The ancient Gnostics called this "repose."

What was really calling me? The same old stuff just messing with me in a new way, or something truly awakening in me that was beyond all that. Sometimes late at night, those long dark nights of the soul as they are sometimes called, I struggled with this dilemma. As time passed, I found out. The voice that became clear and didn't bounce around, but remained at peace with itself I knew was something powerful and great. Not like our issues in life, all those things that run us around and get us balled up in one mess after another, the Spirit's voice calls us to something higher and deeper. That's the best I can do to explain it. I think Jesus' parable is wonderful. It puts into a story the struggle that goes on in each of us. This parable made more and more sense to me the clearer my focus became. Of course! That is what he meant to happen.

Insight 58

> *Jesus said, "Blessed is the man*
> *who has suffered and found life."*

From the Head ...

This insight, like the first noble truth of Buddhism, maintains that life and suffering are together. Suffering is part of the structure. For things to exist, they must suffer. That is the cycle of life: birth, maturity and then death. All our relationships, notions and patterns are determined by this cycle. We love, and the one we love is eventually taken away. We have ideas as to how life should be, and life throws in a monkey wretch. We begin to feel a sense of our separation and alienation from life itself, even though life holds intrigue and wonder. We get caught between our need and our desire. The Buddha taught that suffering could be alleviated through stopping the desire. Jesus called it becoming "passers-by" (Insight 42). Having discovered that life is suffering, a person can move beyond it to something more – the life of the Spirit, or as Jesus called it: "the kingdom of heaven."

To discover one's own suffering does not sound like a blessing. We spend our lives trying as hard as possible to avoid that pain. We create all kinds of psychological and material defense mechanisms. We hedge ourselves around by money, romance, consumerism and the varying array of internal techniques that we practice daily without realizing it. We live unconsciously. We suffer, but we deny it, and keep hoping that things will "work out." It's not until we become honest with ourselves about the truth of existence that something remarkable can happen – the finding of life beyond existence as we commonly experience it. This honesty about existence is the first step toward awareness. Real life, the life of the Spirit, requires great effort on our part to move through our unconscious lives. In later Gnostic texts it is called the "resurrected life," or simply "life," as opposed to the death of mere existence.

From the Heart ...

My father died in May 1968. I was a senior in High School – 17 years old. It was a very painful experience for me. I was in his hospital room when he died. I was so afraid of death that as soon as he passed away, I ran out of the room to my car and drove for hours just trying to escape the feelings. I didn't realize it until much later of course, but that was the definition of my life: trying to escape suffering. Some 20 years later, it occurred to me while doing some therapeutic work, that I had never grieved his loss. I had spent my life running from all the death and decay around me, because I was afraid that if I let the suffering in it would totally destroy me. And, for a time, it felt that way. But the truth was, the moment I began to let the suffering into my awareness I began the journey out of mere existence into the life of the Spirit. I now understand that all spiritual awakening requires a consciousness of suffering.

Spirituality doesn't feel good – that is the "first noble truth" of my knowledge. This awareness is a necessary precursor to a larger awakening. In this way, it is a "blessing" as Jesus suggested. Not that it feels good, or is a great thing in and of itself, but that it leads the way to something beyond it. That has been my experience.

Insight 59

> *Jesus said, "Take heed of the living one*
> *while you are alive, lest you die and seek*
> *to see him and be unable to do so."*

From the Head ...

"Take heed of the living one." When we look at this phrase we might think that Jesus is speaking of himself. That would be an error. Jesus is referring to the Spirit, which is the only true "living one." Everything else is in essence dead. To awaken to the Spirit is to "take heed" of it, and in that awakening to begin the journey toward the fullness to which the Spirit belongs. The idea here is this: without awakening the Spirit remains lost in the cycle of the world. Like a wheel it moves without regard to the suffering that this turning causes. The Spirit is thrown into the world, born and lives a material existence in the darkness, then dies – only to repeat the cycle over and over again. This cycle has no purpose, nor is it a "training ground" as some have suggested. It is just a blind process that requires awakening for the Spirit to leave.

When Jesus says that we are to "take heed" while we are alive, lest we die and are "unable to do so," he is stating the consequence to the unawakened Spirit. One cannot move out of the Spirit's dilemma until the inner work of awareness and awakening occur. This "tak(ing) heed" is a metaphor for the work required to achieve gnosis – the saving knowledge. Since the world is a labyrinth in which the Spirit is trapped, being aware is essential to movement out of that trap.

I have heard it said in recovery groups of one kind or another that insanity is "doing the same thing over and over again expecting different results." In this sense, the Spirit is locked into insanity by its sleep, until awakening moves the Spirit out of the rut. The force of death is so swift that the Spirit cannot awaken fast enough to effectively escape, therefore the Spirit must awaken before death so that the gnosis of the Spirit can step outside of the process immediately after the death of the body.

As complex as all this seems, it boils down to a very simple truth: the awakened Spirit must step out of the process of suffering to return to its home, much like people rafting on a wild river must move out of the stream at a given location or else be drawn into the rapids once again. This, essentially, is what Jesus is suggesting here.

From the Heart ...

"Take heed of the living one," this insight tells me. I have thought about that a great deal. For me it has meant to divorce myself as much as possible from the ordinary reality to which we commonly subscribe without thought or reflection. For the most part, everything we do in the social world is an agreed upon reality designed to constrain and eliminate spiritual truth. It locks us into place and keeps us trapped. I have mentioned this often in my comments on this Gospel.

I suppose what comes up for me here is my exhaustion. The cycle of living in this world, doing the same thing over and over again, has beaten me down a great deal over the lifetimes my Spirit has been reborn. It is not that I remember who or what I was in past lives, although sometimes I have had insights on this level. Rather, I have a knowledge that the cycle has swept me here over and over again, and each time what I was before was swept away, too. It is like going to school and learning a great deal, only to have your mind erased, and having to go back to the same school over again. Of course, having your mind erased means that you are unaware of the dilemma. But just imagine that you find out what is happening. At first you are angry, then frustrated. Finally, you start the effort to not get trapped. That is how I feel. I don't remember my "past lives," but I do have a sense of them. Most of us do on some level. But my awakening is to the truth of who I am, and the process in which I am lost. That is the key thing. That is the beginning of the end, and the beginning of something wonderful and beautiful. That is what this insight tells me.

Insight 60

> They saw a Samaritan carrying a lamb
> on his way to Judea. He said to his disciples,
> "That man is round about the lamb." They said
> to him, "So that he may kill it and eat it."
> He said to them, "While it is alive, he
> will not eat it, but only when he has killed it
> and it has become a corpse." They said to him,
> "He cannot do otherwise." He said to them, "You
> too, look for a place for yourselves within repose,
> lest you become a corpse and be eaten."

From the Head ...

The world swallows the Spirit and consumes it. Jesus, in this insight, uses the analogy of a lamb going to slaughter to make that point. Our True Self, like the lamb, is being lined up for slaughter. The world system uses the Spirit like a seed to grow soul consciousness that is consumed by the forces of the world as an energy dynamic that enlivens the system. Without this slaughtering of the Spirit's production of soul consciousness the world would cease.

As brutal as this sounds, it is the way the material/energy system works. It is a process of consumption to fuel the engine of world dynamics. Spiritual truth does not gloss over this harsh reality. We may seek to deny the harshness of the world, as we often do, but its reality imposes itself on our physical and energy being all the time. The Spirit is trapped in this process, as well, until it awakens to itself as something more and "outside" the realm of the world order.

From the Heart ...

The more I have detached from the everyday world of "normal" reality, the more I see how brutal and harsh it is. Everything is geared to use the energy that is created by the Spirit as a "food" source to fuel the system. Even our social, economic, political and religious institutions become partners in this trap. People just go about their "business" robotically and never really notice that they are being eaten down to their heels. The depression that seems to fill peoples lives more and more is but a symptom of this situation.

As I awakened to this situation and dilemma of the Spirit, I found it critical to spend time away from organized society. It occurred to me that what we have created in our social lives is a matrix of reality that keeps us unaware of what is happening to us. Try to tell somebody about this that isn't awakened, and you find out just how unaware they are. Drones. They live, they work and they die. That's it! I find that kind of unconsciousness quite disturbing now. I view this situation like a farmer planting seeds. When the seeds grow into plants and produce their fruit, the farmer comes and harvests the crop. When people start vibrating at certain energy levels and create large souls, they are ripe for the harvest.

Everything in society is geared to create and foster this situation – unwittingly. The intent of society is to safeguard its members, but in actuality it does the exact opposite. Romantic intrigue and soap opera type lives vibrate our emotional state into a soul pattern that makes it very tasty for the world system. People without awakening hear this and think it is crazy, but everything is geared this way. Everything is consumed as food by something else. Why would we think that our consciousness and soul stuff is not part of that consumption process? It's ignorance, sleep and intoxication. I have seen that the Spirit is the seed, the soul stuff is the harvested fruit. And the seed is just replanted over and over again. If that sounds awful, then so be it. Since nothing, and I mean nothing, gets out of here alive – why would we think that the world is such a lovely place? When we awaken, our Spirit knows better. It knows it belongs to something beyond the tragedy. When we love and care beyond the principles of the world, we tap into the higher truth of that Spirit world. That is why God is spoken of as Love in Christian texts. True love points toward a reality that is far beyond the brutal world in which we physically and energetically live. It has a reality all its own.

This insight, as unglamorous as it seems, drives home the point that most people miss and want to miss; but in missing it, they line themselves up to be recycled back into the system. Jesus practiced rigorous honesty in his teachings, whether it made people comfortable or not. Mostly not, I suspect. I know I need to strive to do that myself.

Insight 61

*Jesus said, "Two will rest on a bed:
the one will die, and the other live." Salome said,
"Who are you, man, that you ... have come up on my
couch and eaten from my table?" Jesus said to her,
"I am he who exists from what is whole.
I was given some of the things of my father."
(Then Salome said), "I am your disciple."
"For this reason I say, if one is whole, one will
be filled with light, but if one is divided
one will be filled with darkness."*

From the Head ...

The patterns of events in the world make little or no sense. "Two will rest on a bed: the one will die, and the other live," makes the point that the world has a random characteristic to it. It is not that one deserves to die and the other deserves to live. The world does not operate with an ethical sensibility to it. It just is the way it is – no reason, nor meaningfulness. For this very reason Gnostics termed the world "deficient." It is deficient in that it has no essential meaningfulness nor moral reason to it.

In many of these insights, where there is a backdrop or context (Salome on her couch), Jesus is often portrayed as an outsider, or intruder. "Who are you, man, that you have come up on my couch and eaten from my table?" evokes a picture of an unwanted guest appearing, but when that guest is "made known" he is immediately given a place of honor as a divine visitation. The insight is that the world of light invades the darkness and at once disturbs us, as expressed in the second insight, and then enlightens us. The revelation that we exist in a world that is fractured is viewed as a divine gift – it is knowledge that one cannot come to without spiritual help.

This insight emphasizes the nature of awakening. It comes from the world of wholeness ("I am he who exists from what is whole"), and descends upon us in an abrupt way. It shows us what we don't see, and then grants wisdom. "Filled with darkness" is like saying "washed in mud" or "filled with emptiness" – oxymorons. The world is like that – something that seems one way, but is in actuality another. To awaken you have to see beyond the context of the world into spiritual reality – a reality that is often referred to as "wholeness" in these insights.

From the Heart . . .

My brother was 19 years old when he was killed in an automobile accident. He and three other boys were coming back from college late one night and their car skidded into a telephone pole. The driver and the front seat passenger (my brother) were killed. One rear seat passenger was severely injured, but survived, and the other was thrown free and escaped without a scratch. When I got the call I was asleep. The person on the other end of the phone told me, "There's no easy way to say this – your brother is dead." I thought, as you might imagine, that it was a prank call at first, but as the sleep left my eyes and head, I was wracked with the pain of this loss. I wanted it to make sense somehow, but it never did. Just an accident. There were some facts associated with it, but no meaning.

I was in seminary at the time, and I used this event to really push me into my quest for truth, or at least meaning. I found only suffering. Ironically, the boy that escaped without a scratch came by to visit me one day. He was hardly able to look me in the eyes, and I wondered what was going on. He cried, and finally asked me if I would forgive him. I asked, "Why? What did you do that needs my forgiveness?" He said simply, "I lived." I was dumbfounded, and just hugged him. I told him that I was glad that he lived, and that his death would not make the death of my brother okay or meaningful to me. He left, and I have not seen him since. Perhaps he needed to hear that from me. But it was a powerful moment, one that comes back to me every now and then.

"Two will rest on a bed: one will die and the other live." Yes, and we are left trying to make sense of it. It makes no external sense, and all we are left with is the internal wrestling that existence brings. The boy who lived was an abrupt visitation for me. I have had many such visitations, and I am quite sure there will be more. Each time they bring me to the fracture in the world, and push me beyond it.

Insight 62

> Jesus said, "It is to those who are worthy of my mysteries that I tell my mysteries. Do not let your left hand know what your right hand is doing."

From the Head ...

Is it possible to keep your "left hand from know(ing) what your right hand is doing?" Not in the literal sense. But this insight pushes us beyond the literal, and forces us to view the left and right hands as aspects of ourselves. More often than we realize, something is happening in us that our conscious mind is unaware of. We often do things that are unexplainable – even by ourselves. Invisible issues can easily drive us into patterns of behavior and thinking that seem to have no source. They do, of course, but we cannot see them, and often takes years to uncover their origin. So, when Jesus asks us the keep knowledge from one part of ourselves, it is something that we are very accustomed to doing in actuality.

I think of this insight like this: my spiritual "doing" doesn't make sense to my biological and social being, and frequently by deferring to that spiritual aspect of myself, I have to move away from the drives that seek to force my life into common patterns. It is very much like keeping my left hand from knowing what my right hand is doing, which I find to be a rather humorous saying at this point.

Being "worthy" of the mysteries is simply being someone who desires to hear them. Most people don't, and don't wish to be "bothered" by spiritual talk. They are not worthy of it. It is not a moral judgment, just a practical one. Each person determines his own "worthiness" by his openness. How closed are we? How bound to social convention and common reality are we? These are issues that this insight raises for us to think about. How willing are we to risk not letting our left hand not know what our right hand is doing? Jesus makes you think.

From the Heart ...

I am very aware that I live in two very distinct worlds – a world of invisible movement and enchantment, and a world of fixed notions and social realities. Even as those worlds overlap, they are quite separate realities, and to see them clearly I have to practice what this insight suggests: keeping them distinct from one another.

Recently I was demonstrating the fluidity of consciousness to someone by asking them to "focus their consciousness on their left foot." I told them: "See, a moment ago 'you' were elsewhere, now you are in your foot." They laughed, but they could see my point – which was merely that consciousness has a fluidity to it. We become so stuck that we think of ourselves as only existing in a certain kind of way, or in a certain place. To "not let your left hand know what your right hand is doing" is to practice fluidity of consciousness.

At this point in my life, I see that my "doing" in the world, and my "being" in the world are two different things. My "being" is not, strictly speaking, what I do at all. My "doing" (social and economic routines, etc.) is quite separate from the reality of my "being." While this may sound confusing, it isn't. I am more than the sum of all my doings and roles and whatever else may be visibly factual about my life. I could say, as with this insight, that often my left hand doesn't know what my right hand is "doing."

Insight 63

Jesus said, "There was a rich man who had much money. He said, 'I shall put my money to use so that I may sow, reap, plant, and fill my storehouse with produce, with the result that I shall lack nothing.' Such were his intentions, but that same night he died. Let him who has ears hear."

From the Head ...

This story appears in the public Gospels as well, although in a slightly different form. In the Gospel of Thomas the "rich man" is an investor, whereas in the public Gospels he is a "farmer." This insight is not a "moralization" as it is in the public Gospels (the farmer is called a "fool!"). Here the point is more subtle and leads one to internal awareness, not external moralizations about "riches." Our "intentions" to make the world function on some kind of rational and consistent basis are illusory, Jesus suggests. It is not "wrong" to want to invest money to make life easier; the problem arises with expectations of control.

Another aspect of this insight that is important is the idea of investing identity into something that will ease the pain of feeling the emptiness of the world. It is a common mistake of spiritual "ignorance" and "sleep" to think that something we "do" in this world can make our homesickness and emptiness go away so we will "lack nothing." The world is the embodiment of emptiness, if you will. To think that some behavior, investment, person or accomplishment will make that go away is simply illusion. To be sure, the world has a way of telling us that the emptiness is because we are deficient and to blame, and if we could just be smarter, more moral and faithful all our "lack" would dissolve. This lie is underneath most activities on the social, political and economic level, but it is just that – a lie. The world itself is empty and void of any real truth and loving essence. Anyone who has invested "in the world" with expectations that it would pay off in meaningfulness and wholeness has discovered the "death" that comes quickly on the heels of such actions and beliefs. This short parable makes clear the point that the world cannot be managed into something that it is not – even with all our intelligence and craft.

From the Heart ...

There's an old saying: "The road to hell is paved with good intentions." I've experienced the truth of this many times in my life. The "good intentions" may have legitimate aims, and be worthy of our efforts, but we end up with a handful of nothing.

There is a story that Carlos Castaneda tells of a time he was walking down a street with Don Juan. Along the way Carlos spots a snail crawling out of a flower bed onto the sidewalk, and without thought he picked it up and placed it back into the garden, thinking that he had done a "good deed." Don Juan asked him why he did such a thing. Carlos explained that the snail belonged in the garden and was in danger out on the sidewalk, so he was just helping him out. Don Juan told him that perhaps the snail was fleeing some predator in the flower bed and he had just placed the snail into the jaws of death, instead of actually helping him. Carlos was stunned by this revelation and reached to pull the snail out of the flower bed, whereas Don Juan stopped him and said, "Leave him alone – it was his destiny to be messed with by a stupid man."

This story impacted me, because I could see that many of my good intentions were mindless, and were based on no real knowledge, only guesses as to the nature and meaning of some event or action. I came to see that my assumptions about the world and the beings that move through it are something to be overcome. Because of the nature of the world itself, the good that I wish to do more often than not turns into a nightmare.

This insight forced me to examine my assumptions, and cautioned me to walk lightly through the world. If I began to believe that my investments in the world would pay off with meaningful results, then I would get trapped into the matrix of the system that is "death" to the Spirit. Who I am, and the essence of what will make me "lack for nothing" is not of this world at all.

Insight 64

Jesus said, "A man had received visitors.
And when he had prepared the dinner, he sent
his servant to invite the guests. He went to the first
one and said to him, 'My master invites you.'
He said, 'I have claims against some merchants.
They are coming to me this evening. I must go and
give them my orders. I ask to be excused from the
dinner.' He went to another and said to him,
'My master has invited you.' He said to him,
'I have just bought a house and am required for the day.
I shall not have any spare time.' He went to another
and said to him, 'My master invites you.'
He said to him, 'My friend is going to get married,
and I am to prepare the banquet. I shall not be able to
come. I ask to be excused from the dinner.' He went to
another and said to him, 'My master invites you.'
He said to him, 'I have just bought a farm, and I am on
my way to collect the rent. I shall not be able to come.
I ask to be excused.' The servant returned and said
to his master, 'Those whom you invited to the dinner
have asked to be excused.' The master said to his servant,
'Go outside to the streets and bring back those whom
you happen to meet, so that they may dine.' Businessmen
and merchants will not enter the places of my father."

From the Head ...

Every excuse in this parable is legitimate. Business, family and
friends place demands on our time. Who would say, for instance, that

159

a person who was chosen to be the Best Man at a wedding should skip his duties to go to a separate dinner party given elsewhere? And yet, this insight suggests that all obligations in the world are unimportant when it comes to matters of the Spirit. If we make the things of the world important, we miss the truth of who we are and what we are truly invited to participate in.

Look how bogged down we can become. Everything gets in our way, and we fall asleep to our true calling – which is always the call from the Spirit to discover our True Self. Business, family and friends are all distractions that must be placed in perspective if we are to attain authentic awareness.

This parable becomes a list of things that get in the way. It's meant to be humorous. It just goes on and on. Anything, if we let it, becomes more important than that which is truly important. Like so many of Jesus' parables and insight, this teaching is meant to remind us of what we already know: there is only one important thing – the Spirit!

From the Heart ...

A dear friend who was dying of AIDS invited me to dinner one night. I was swamped with work, and so I declined. At the time I felt badly, and I even thought to myself – perhaps you should go, you never know. But, I ignored that voice, and went back to work. A few weeks later, I found out that my friend had died. He took his own life at a predetermined time since he didn't wish to put his friends and family through the ordeal of dying of AIDS. He had eaten dinner with all of his friends individually to say goodbye. I will never forget having excused myself from his invitation, and ignoring that voice inside of me that told me to go.

When the Spirit calls, it is important to listen and act. I have learned to pay closer attention to that voice that speaks quietly and softly. Call it intuition or the Spirit, it is always a voice to be followed – even at the risk of ignoring earthly obligations and arrangements. I always learn the hard way – like most of us.

Insight 65

He said, "There was a good man who owned a vineyard. He leased it to tenant farmers so that they might work it and he might collect the produce from them. He sent his servant so that the tenants might give him the produce of the vineyard. They seized his servant and beat him, all but killing him. The servant went back and told his master. The master said, 'Perhaps he did not recognize them.' He sent another servant. The tenants beat this one as well. Then the owner sent his son and said, 'Perhaps they will show respect to my son.' Because the tenants knew that it was he who was the heir to the vineyard, they seized him and killed him. Let him who has ears hear."

From the Head ...

This parable also appears in various forms in the public Gospels. The orthodox slant is that the world is the vineyard "leased" to mankind who have stolen it from its rightful owner – God, the creator. But this is not the point in this insight. Since the world is not viewed as a "good place," but as a "corpse," the vineyard can only be understood as the "fullness" or "pleroma" – which is the Gnostic word for Spiritual reality. In this parable, the vineyard is being usurped by agents that deny the productivity to the larger whole – the "good man." (In later Gnostic thinking, the word "man" is understood to be also the true name of God – so Jesus is titled: the son of man.)

The agents, or "powers" as St. Paul called them, attempt to keep knowledge away from those that rightfully belong to the fullness.

The produce that is to be retrieved is the lost Spirit in the world, but the powers of the world attempt to keep that "produce" to itself.

There is no ordinary moralism in this parable, precisely because it was told to illustrate the predicament that mankind finds itself in: trapped in a system usurped by powers that murder and destroy to maintain control. In this fashion, the world and the powers of that "creation" are at war with the fullness that is seeking its lost "produce." As is typical of Jesus, he ends this parable by asking people to really "hear," and underscores the dilemma of mankind in a clear and understandable manner.

From the Heart ...

Most of us want to imagine that we are surrounded by goodness, and that if we are good people ourselves, that goodness will save us. But it won't. What "saves" is a combination of personal enlightenment and awakening, coupled with the activity of the spiritual fullness that is always moving to retrieve us from the darkness.

A part of awakening is the ability to see that there is another reality at work that comes not from this world, but from beyond it. It is like a reality that touches people without their knowing it (unless they are awake!), and moves in strange ways among us like a force collecting its produce. But there is a counter force acting, as well. It is a force that keeps us asleep, ignorant, distracted and diverted from the larger truth.

I try to spend time each day observing my own focus, and seeing where I am spiritually. This meditative time can be a moment of reflection or contemplation, or it can be writing or talking with a friend, but whatever it is, it must be done with a conscious intent to stay free from the power(s) of the world. I find that a great deal of spirituality is discipline. Awakening must be cultivated like fine produce from a wonderful vineyard.

Insight 66

Jesus said, "Show me the stone which the builders have rejected. That one is the cornerstone."

From the Head ...

This saying, which appears in the public Gospels as well, has long been perceived by orthodox believers to reference Jesus himself, who in this insight is represented by the "rejected" stone. But like all of Jesus' insights in this secret and private listing of teachings, there is a deeper meaning.

A "cornerstone" is the most important building block of an expanding structure. It holds in place all others, and must be beautiful as it is easily seen. The "rejected" stone that is the actual cornerstone, of course, is the spiritual reality that is ignored by the world's powers.

In Gnostic thinking, the world's creation comes from an error, or ignorance of the divine fullness. Creating a hardened reality that thereby fixes suffering into a place, the ignorant creator rejects the dynamic love, tenderness and spiritual reality of the divine whole-ness. Jesus says, "Show me the stone which the builders have rejected" referring to the creator God and his host of "powers" that reject the larger reality of the divine fullness in favor of their own created world in which a lost spark of the divine is held captive.

Short and to the point, this insight asks us to see the true essence of our being. To "show" the stone is to reveal the spiritual truth of being, something that Jesus was always compelling his disciples to do. I imagine that there was a long pause between the two sentences in this insight. Jesus asked: "Show me the stone" referring to the (listener's) spiritual truth, and after the spiritual reality was revealed he would say, "that is the cornerstone."

From the Heart ...

As I was writing about this insight, I became aware of how often in my life I ignored a larger truth for something that distracted my attention. It is our common dilemma, I suppose. In the public Gospels it has Jesus saying, we strain at a 'gnat' and swallow a 'camel.' That's me, more often than I care to mention.

Most of the time the issue I thought was bothering me, wasn't it at all, but something beyond it. Just like most of my religious life was about the small God that I was always trying to explain, rather than a "fullness" beyond. We commonly "reject" the real cornerstone of something, rather than face it squarely and see the truth of it. It's a powerful thing to be asked by a true friend, "What's behind that?" We can be upset, angry or frustrated, but we need to ask ourselves (or be asked!): what's really happening?

Like most of us, I get bogged down paying bills (or trying to), running around "doing my life" and living in "forgetfulness" about my own spiritual reality. I "reject" it without even thinking. I try to remember to ask myself: "Who am I?" That's like saying, "Show me the rejected stone." When I remember who I really am, it's like saying: "That is the cornerstone."

Insight 67

Jesus said, "If anyone who knows the ALL still feels a personal deficiency, he is completely deficient."

From the Head ...

Knowing your True Self and feeling deficient are contradictions. To know who you truly are is to dissolve deficiency, so if you feel deficient, then your knowledge of self is deficient. This is not a criticism or moral judgment, but a deep truth about reality itself. I see this insight very much like the old saying, "you cannot be a little bit pregnant." You either are, or you are not. That is the essence here.

The "ALL" I put in capital letters because it expresses the idea of the divine fullness, or the larger spiritual reality to which we ultimately belong. Knowing the "ALL" dissolves the "personal" in the way in which we ordinarily understand individuality. Our "feel(ings)" are a part of an illusory meaning. In other words, our feelings, ordinary thoughts and drives, are all part of a deficient world, and so to "feel" that deficiency is to live within its matrix.

From the Heart ...

We often confuse "personal integrity" or "personal responsibility" with spirituality. They are not the same. Integrity and responsibility are all part of an illusory meaning. That is not to say that we shouldn't assume responsibility or have integrity in our walking through the world, but we must understand that these ideas are all part of something that is itself devoid of ultimate meaningfulness.

I have found that the world itself is a kind of "lie." It's rather humorous that we would talk so much about those who are liars without seeing the larger lie. So, everything becomes a kind of lie. Living an ordinary life is the biggest lie of all. So, those who claim to be the most moral, are in truth, the most filled with the lie of the world. I find that ironic, if not a bit laughable.

For me, authentic integrity and responsibility have to do with the "ALL," and not this world, which forces shame, guilt and terror on us to keep us controlled and locked into place. I believe that it is often valuable to "lie to the liar" to avoid the trap of the lie. In my detachment from the force of the world, this ironic situation has become more and more apparent. Everything in this world has as a backdrop this irony. Whenever I feel like a stranger in this world, I begin to see that it is important to get in touch with that as an ally. To be a stranger in a strange world is to say, my home is elsewhere. If I stay with my strangeness in the strange world, I lose touch with that to which the strangeness is pointing. I never let go, and I never get home. I just feel strange all the time, and literally become a part of the strange world itself.

I think it was Kierkegaard who alluded to the fact that to be viewed as insane in an insane world is an act of sanity. Amen.

Insight 68

> Jesus said, "Blessed are you when you are hated and persecuted. Wherever you have been persecuted they will find no place."

From the Head ...

Being hated and persecuted certainly aren't wonderful feelings, nor are they issues that we would intentionally seek out, but here Jesus is saying they are a "bless(ing)." The most fundamental reason for this teaching is the truth that spirituality doesn't feel good, nor does it create safety in the world. Quite the contrary, authentic spirituality puts us at odds with the illusory reality of the world, and strips bare the false essence of the social consensual order. The "bless(ing)" is knowing the truth, a truth that sets one free but also can make life in this world more difficult.

Finding a "place" refers to finding a resting spot, or being able to let down your defenses. In saying that "wherever you have been persecuted they will find no place," Jesus is simply teaching that the obsession with suffering that occurs in this material reality offers no place of repose – either for those who are persecuted or for those that do the persecuting. It is hellish.

From the Heart ...

To awaken to the Spirit is to risk being rejected and vilified. Why? Because you cease to fit in neatly with what the world is all about. But I discovered that even though that is true, awakening also holds a vision and experience of something beyond and greater than anything the world has to offer. Every time I was hated or talked about, I reminded myself that the spiritual reality to which I belonged was my true home, and not the world that was attacking me.

To be honest, there are times that it is hard for me to see that my awakening is a blessing. I think that goes with the territory. But the deeper truth is that without knowing your True Self, the world is worse – for not knowing that you belong to something greater creates the fear that defines ordinary life. We get trapped. It is hell, indeed.

Insight 69

Jesus said, "Blessed are they who have been persecuted within themselves. It is they who have truly come to know the father and mother of light. Blessed are the hungry, for the belly of him who desires will be filled."

From the Head ...

Most people tell me that they never felt like they "fit in." All their lives, they say, they felt as if they didn't belong here, or felt like outsiders to their family, social structures, and even their own friends. It's nothing they can put their finger on, they say, just a deeply held feeling or knowledge.

The term for this is alienation – a universal phenomenon of being in the world. By and large we treat this alien sense as if it were a psychological problem, with a psychological answer. Almost everything we do as human beings is a result of attempting to overcome this terrible sense of feeling alien, but we never do. Most of us never even became conscious of what is going on within ourselves – we just avoid it with all our psychological might.

This insight is very powerful and illuminating, because it speaks directly to the human condition, and clearly teaches that our alienation, here spoken of as being "persecuted within," is a special knowledge if we would just "desire (to be) filled" by it. We each already know the truth, a truth that we avoid as if it were our deepest problem, when in fact it is our only answer. We feel alien because something in us is in fact alien. When that alien spark is known – the father and mother of light is known. Knowing your True Self is knowledge of God. That is Jesus' message.

From the Heart ...

Many years ago I was visiting some folks in Alabama. One afternoon I decided to walk the little town square, and just sit and enjoy the "southern flavor" of the area. Actually, I was a little "down" – just one of those blue days that seem to come on us for no apparent reason. After walking the square, I sat down on a park bench to rest and watch people. Presently, an old guy, like someone out of a '50s sitcom, sat next to me. We acknowledged each other, and then stared off. We just sat quietly for probably ten minutes or so. Then the old man just shook his head as if having pondered something and finally given up, and said, "All God's children got problems." He got up, and just walked off. I chuckled to myself wondering whether he was referring to me specifically on this occasion, or all the folks he saw walking by going about their daily business. Both, I concluded.

"All God's children got problems," stuck in my head over the years. I saw that it was true, for indeed, all of us live in a world of hurt and pain. But even in the good times, I reckoned, those "problems" continued, and wasn't just because things weren't going my way. There was something in me that just couldn't get comfortable with living here.

I think all of us feel that way. Some are better at defending themselves from this strange sense of discomfort, while others of us just fall apart over and over again, never really knowing what to do about it. Well, of course, there is nothing we can "do" about it. All our "doing" doesn't change it, even though we wish that it would.

This inner discomfort, as I put it, is the classic alienation that philosophers and psychologists write about. I have felt it all my life. So have you, if you're honest with yourself, and look closely enough. As I read this insight, I recognize that the "persecuted within" that Jesus is talking about is the inner discomfort I have always felt, and I see now that it has been a "blessing," because it pushed me to see its truth – that something of me belongs to something greater. Like a small voice, it has spoke to me since my birth, and now like a letter from home, I open it to read of my origin. I think this is what this insight is about. It's one of my favorites.

Insight 70

Jesus said, "That which you have will save you if you bring it forth from yourselves. That which you do not have within you will kill you if you do not have it within you."

From the Head ...

This insight, much like the previous one, suggests that inner content, not external forms, is the essential truth of who we are. Trying to be what you are not is murderous to the truth of self. The world (both social and biological), with all its pressure of conformity, seeks to mold us into "beings of the world," instead of "beings in the world." This distinction is the most relevant issue here, for "bring(ing) forth" from our innermost self provides us with a sense of being that distances us from all the conforming pressures that the world creates.

There are all kinds of practical applications to this insight. Life is more joyous and wonderful when we are free to experience our True Self, for as this insight intimates, there is such inner beauty that we can scarcely imagine it without bring it forth and letting it live all around us. It is saving, since it saves us from the small, hurtful reality in which we commonly find ourselves. Our lives are literally a lie without this "bring(ing) forth" of this innermost truth. As Thoreau put it: "The mass of men lead lives of quiet desperation." Bringing forth this desperation with life volume, places us above and beyond the scope of the mundane world, and lifts us to who we truly are.

From the Heart ...

"To thine own self be true." Yes, but what is my "own self," and what are all the false selves created for me? This distinction is what pushed me into crisis many times in my life. I lived most of my life thinking I was someone I wasn't – like most of us. Then, at crisis times I would say, "I'm not that, I'm this!" And, I lived between "this" and "that" most of my life. I came to realize that I was neither "this" nor "that," but rather I was the being beyond the this and that life I was leading which was disturbed by the whole thing.

Monoimos, an early Arab Gnostic, wrote this:

"Cease to seek after God and creation and things like these and seek after yourself of yourself, and learn who it is who appropriates all things within you without exception and says, "My God, my mind, my thought, my soul, my body," and learn whence comes grief, and rejoicing and love and hatred, and waking without intention, and sleeping without intention, and anger without intention, and love without intention. And if you carefully consider these things, you will find yourself within yourself, being both one and many like that stroke, and will find the outcome of yourself."

"That which you have will save you if you bring it forth from yourselves." That is Jesus' wisdom here. Monoimos echoed it beautifully in the above discourse. It is when I cease to look outside myself for the answer to who I am, that it can come forth from within me. It was so simple, it evaded me.

Insight 71

*Jesus said, "I shall destroy this house,
and no one will be able to build it (again)."*

From the Head ...

This saying, which occurs as a reference to the temple in Jerusalem in the public Gospels, it not meant that way here. "This house" represents the world, which to Jesus was built without agreement from the fullness, and stands as an error and must be dissolved. He dissolves it by denying its ultimacy, and seeing it as deficient and a false reality. Once this takes place in a person, it cannot be re-built, since its falseness is then known.

From the Heart ...

You can't un-know what you know. Once you see through the veil of falseness that surrounds us, you can never feel the same way, nor think the same thoughts as you did before. This realization has caused people to believe that "ignorance is bliss," which is a falsehood the world would like us to believe.

When my son was about seven years old, one night just before going to bed he asked: "Is God real?" This question came on the heels of his coming to the knowledge that Santa Claus was a story told to children, and had no essential reality other than in some "make-believe" way. Was God like that, too, he was asking. I told him, in good spiritual tradition, that I would answer that for him if he would answer a question for me first. He agreed. I asked, "Is love real?" He said, "Of course." I said, "Show me love. Where is it that I can look at it?" He was puzzled, and finally said, "Well, I guess I can't. I don't know where it is." I told him that the God of love and light was real, but I could not show him, since God doesn't exist in the way we understand existence. "I know it," I told him, "but I can't show you – except in my telling." He smiled, thankfully – since that was the best answer I had – and drifted off to sleep as I lay there marveling at his question.

I don't think of the world, or God, or anything for that matter, the way I use to. I can't, and never will again. But what I have come to is so much more, why would I want to go back? That is what this insight says to me

Insight 72

> *A man said to him, "Tell my brothers to divide*
> *my father's possessions with me." He said to him,*
> *"O man, who has made me a divider?" He turned to his*
> *disciples and said to them, "I am not a divider, am I?"*

From the Head . . .

Division, separation and polarization are all aspects and powers within the world. Jesus, by identifying himself with the "fullness" says of himself, "I am not a divider," which asserts his belonging to the world of wholeness and unity, rather than the divided world of "creation."

This is an important insight for us to digest, since it requires us, as all these insights do, to think of ourselves in different terms. When Jesus turns to his disciples and says, "I am not a divider, am I?" he is asking them to make the same statement about themselves.

Our world is disconnected and split into opposites. Earlier in Insight 22, when Jesus tells us to "make the two one," he is referring to dissolving the disunity the world creates, and move our true being back into the "fullness." And, since the Spirit trapped here has been shattered into many sparks, he also speaks of this as an activity that must be accomplished in the world, not just inside of ourselves.

This also reminds me of Jesus' public Gospel admonition not to judge, since a judgmental way of life feeds into the world system of things. Jesus makes this point in many different ways, but with the same point. It is from the fullness which we come, and it is to the fullness that we are to proceed.

From the Heart ...

Jesus taught publicly that we should love our neighbors as we do ourselves. He even went so far as to say that we should love our enemies. The reason for this is stated in this insight: it dissolves division, and helps us see that we are many aspects of the same thing, and that the hardened forms in the world that appear as opposites, are in truth only one thing.

This has been a very difficult thing for me to get. How can something be many things and yet be only one thing? This is true of the Spirit trapped in this world, a world that separates and divides through its hardness and physical process. It is really one, but appears as many.

When I look deeply at this issue, I begin to see myself in others, and in all of life. In a very real way, all life is me, and I am all life. The hardness around the life is what is an "artificial" separation and division. The hardness is the "darkness," and the unity is the "light." That's the best I can do to say what I see.

This insight has made a difference in how I relate to others, and to life around me. When I do something to others, I do it to myself. Jesus was publicly and privately very clear on this matter, as has been every enlightened and awakened being. It is from the fullness that we have come, and to that fullness we return. That is the strength of knowledge.

Insight 73

Jesus said, "The harvest is great but the laborers are few. Beseech the lord, therefore, to send out laborers to the harvest."

From the Head ...

The idea of harvest has as a backdrop the idea of judgment – harvest is a gathering of good crops, and the throwing away of the bad. This judgment concept is alien to Jesus, and so we must look elsewhere for the meaning of this insight. When I think of the harvest as being awakened to the True Self, this insight makes perfect sense for Jesus to have said it.

Awakening to the truth of one's inner being jars a person into a great disturbance, and is very disconcerting. For this reason, spiritual leaders have often taught that having a guide through the process is best – even though it is not necessary. To have someone be with you as your awakening unfolds is a great gift, but few are able to do the work. If there were a "priestly" role in Jesus' teaching, this would be it. A "laborer" in this sense is a co-journeyer, who is sometimes a guide, and other times just a companion.

From the Heart ...

As I have written previously, I have had many guides along my way. I attribute them with having brought me great insights as to what I was seeing. They never created what I saw, nor gave me precise definitions, but they tended me as I struggled to understand what was happening. I, in my struggle, helped them as well. That is the way it works.

To be honest, I see myself as a "laborer" in the harvest of awakening that I see occurring all around me. It is the only real "job" that we have – everything else is just mundane and ultimately unimportant. Whatever we do to make our way through this world, our real task is to awaken and help others in their awakening.

But there's also a catch – a true laborer doesn't demand ownership. In other words, you help someone as best you can, and then you let them move on. So, being a guide is always a "walking with" until the time that "walking alone" occurs. Then, as a laborer must, you move on to the next "harvest."

Insight 74

He said, "O lord, there are many around the
drinking trough, but there is nothing in the cistern."

From the Head ...

The imagery of water is often used as a metaphor for the Spirit. This insight is an example of Jesus telling his friends that many people are looking in the wrong place for the truth of themselves. My sense is that this insight has to do with "religious" people, who tend to make their rituals and particular context a thing to be worshipped, instead of doing the hard inner work that is required by a spiritual awakening.

Jesus was fond of poking fun of religious types – not to judge them or ridicule them, but to make them see that their theatrics are just psychodrama, and nothing more. He called them "blind guides," or "white washed sepulchers, all clean and white on the outside, but filled with dead men's bones." The picture of people trying to drink from a dry well falls within this domain.

From the Heart ...

It occurs to me that all major religions began in desert areas. Desert people knew better than most, I suppose, the difference between brown and green: one meant life, the other death. It was clear and simple. An oasis was green since it had water; everything else was death. So, in religion water becomes an important image. The Spirit is "green" since it is true life, and everything else is "brown." Having spent time in the desert this imagery becomes quite illuminating and instructive.

When I look at my life's journey, I see that it had been a series of "dry wells," until I stopped looking "around" for the answer and started digging within. But even when you dig within you can dig a dry well. Knowing where to dig, and what to look for, becomes critical to spirituality. You have to dig deep enough to get to the Spirit. If you dig too shallow a well, you get only the psychological stuff. That's not the Spirit. All one has to do is just look around and see that many people are offering "dry wells" as if they are filled with water. "False prophets" they are sometimes called.

Once I had two Jehovah Witnesses come to my door. I invited them in. As they sat down, I told them that I would like to hear from their hearts what they thought and knew to be true without quoting scripture. I assured them I was very well read in the Bible and would catch them if they did, and that they would have to leave. I told them, "I want to hear your soul's talk." Our session lasted about one minute. They were so externalized and memorized, that they had no real life to them. Robots! Dry wells.

I'm not writing this to be judgmental, but rather to illuminate the difference between a dry well and a person of Spirit. A person of Spirit can reveal the "soul's talk" easily and without fear. Ask and you shall receive: a person of Spirit will never be bothered by your request to hear them speak of it, nor will they need to quote some book. They will be "green" and not "brown."

Insight 75

*Jesus said, "Many are standing at the door, but
it is the solitary who will enter the bridal chamber."*

From the Head ...

Group conformity, social consensual agreement and mass
mentality are not spirituality. You meet the Spirit in individuals who
have moved apart from the social matrix and found the depth of the
Spirit as their source of identity. It is the "solitary" who enter.

The imagery of the "bridal chamber" has significance in later
Gnostic thinking. It may have originated with Jesus here in this
insight, although most scholars would no doubt say that this is a
saying placed in Jesus' mouth. I'm not so sure. A bridal chamber is a
place where a marriage takes place, and the union is made sacred. It
requires a serious mind and a loving heart, and can only be entered
into alone to meet one's partner. In Gnostic churches the bridal
chamber became a ritual of uniting with the Spirit, although little is
known about the content and nature of this activity.

Once again Jesus is making the point that spirituality is serious
work, and no one can do it for you. You must do your own inner
examination and digging. To marry the Spirit is to put aside all other
identification, and to place that spiritual reality at the core of all life,
where it rightfully belongs.

From the Heart ...

Jesus' family thought he was crazy. I'm sure he felt alone and
isolated from everything he had grown up with. I relate to that, as

anyone who has awakened spiritually can. I literally feel "wedded" to something that is pushing and pulling me beyond all my concepts and notions, into a reality of Spirit. So, I'm not surprised by imagery of a "bridal chamber."

Spiritual truth costs something in this world. It costs you fitting in, sometimes even being respected. But then again, it's not a loss, since everything other than the Spirit has a kind of falseness to it anyway.

Being "solitary" isn't the same as being alone really. It is being aware of one's inner truth, separate from the crowd mentality that dictates reality, and places one in a larger context beyond conventional notions. It's like the old adage: you can't see the forest for the trees. Until you step back enough, you can't see where you are. You just wander around bumping into things. This type of insight, like this one in number 75, always help me get clarity when I am feeling a bit out of sorts with the world. After all, why wouldn't I? I am living a "solitary" life, separate from the common reality of the world. That's wonderful! Like a wedding celebration.

Insight 76

*Jesus said, "The kingdom of the (Spirit) is like a
merchant who had a consignment of merchandise
and who discovered a pearl. That merchant was shrewd.
He sold the merchandise and bought the pearl
alone for himself. You, too, seek (the Spirit's)
unfailing and enduring treasure where no moth
comes near to devour and no worm destroys."*

From the Head ...

The "pearl" is symbolic of the Spirit or spark of the divine. We are all merchants, who spend our time buying into the reality of the world. Then, we discover something else going on inside of us. It is the "pearl" stirring. Jesus says, sell the old reality and buy the pearl! That is the only smart (shrewd!) thing to do. It is priceless, whereas everything else is just junk.

Thomas, sometime later in a separate work, writes a story titled: "The Hymn of the Pearl." Its theme surrounds the Spirit's entrapment in the world by a serpent, and its retrieval by a divine emissary (the redeemer) who gets lost, but then recovers his true identity and task. It is one of the most beautiful of spiritual writings, that is meant to illuminate who we are as divine Spirits, and not just "garments" of this world.

Many of Jesus' sayings revolve around the image of a pearl, not only because a pearl is beautiful, but because it is formed out of a grain of sand (an irritant inside the shell of a clam) that becomes something so beautiful that it eclipses all the outer trappings of the shell. It's just one of those metaphors that work in describing spiritual awakening: an irritant that becomes everything valuable.

183

Again, like in the previous insight, Jesus tells us that the merchant (us) must buy the pearl for ourselves. He calls it a "shrewd" decision, because it cannot be "devour(ed)" or "destroyed." The opposite is true as well. It is literally stupid to miss what is valuable and settle for what is junk, that will be devoured and destroyed by the world.

From the Heart ...

The merchant who sold everything to buy the pearl really strikes home with me. I find myself using it in reference to many things in life. I tell my son, for instance, to not spend his money on junk, but on things he really wants and needs. I tell him the story of the pearl, and he just looks at me, like any 10 year old would, and thinks his old dad is weird. But, he remembers it. It's just one of those stories that sticks in our psyche because it has so much essential truth to it.

The classic image of someone "selling their soul" or just losing their soul, is one that also sticks in our psyches. Sadly, of course, most people have sold themselves for a job, or for comfort in some manner, and never given the matter much thought as to what they have bought for a great price. Most people are slaves who no longer have a self, just robotic motions and shallow dramas to keep them occupied as they line up to feed the world system. Little wonder that Jesus told a parable like this one. We are merchants and merchandise all rolled into one.

Insight 77

Jesus said, "It is I who am the light which is above them all. It is I who am the all. From me did the all come forth, and unto me did the all extend. Split a piece of wood, and I am there. Lift up the stone, and you will find me there."

From the Head ...

At first reading this insight would seem rather uncharacteristic of Jesus, since it seems to exalt himself in a way that is unusual of his basic teachings. However, when viewed from the focus of these insights as they are collected in the Gospel of Thomas, it makes much more sense. The point is: the Spirit existed before anything came into manifest being.

Jesus is teaching in this insight what each of us must come to understand about ourselves, that the light within us is the light that is above all other light.

This insight, therefore, is like hearing the Spirit speak within ourselves. Even though the earthly Jesus is speaking these words to other earthly beings, the source of the words comes from elsewhere, and is intended to reach that in each of us that comes from elsewhere. It is not a statement about Jesus' exaltation, but rather a proclamation from the Spirit to the Spirit. It is an awakening insight, like a wake-up call, meant to work upon the Spirit to come to its self-realization.

Unfortunately, it is teachings like these, when mis-understood, that create religious myopia about Jesus. It is clear from the focus and thrust of these insights, that Jesus did not intend to create a religion around himself, or some kind of personal theology about his human life. Rather, his intention was to awaken the Spirit within. After all, that is the point of saying, "Split a piece of wood, and I am there. Lift up a stone, and you will find me there." The truth is always inside and under, never on the surface of things, he is teaching.

I find this teaching to be very significant, as it becomes a statement that can be made to oneself with regard to the world. Who we are, Jesus is saying, is from beyond all space and time, from a world that was before existence could be reckoned. It is that knowledge that begins to awaken the Spirit that Jesus, as the Christ, feels drawn to retrieve.

From the Heart ...

This insight has had an impact on me. I think in and of itself it is an awakening agent that has a kind of "energy" that calls to the innermost part of a person. When I first read it years ago, I had to read it over and over again. It just wouldn't let go of me. It became a beacon from a world that my Spirit knew, but my psyche could not quite grasp. I discovered that, indeed, the light from beyond was "under" every stone I picked up, and every piece of wood I cut in two. In others words, having been awakened, I saw it everywhere under the surface of the ordinary.

I remember in a church service telling people that "I was the light beyond the light," and how uncomfortable that made them. I told them not to look at it as if it were something strange and narcissistic, but something they could see in themselves as well. Of course, we are so trained to think of ourselves as merely "created" creatures, imperfect and sinners – "short of the glory of God." But our Spirit is part of God, and in the Spirit there is no distance and no difference. To say, as Jesus did here, "it is I who am the all," is to simply say I and the Spirit are one and the same. If we do not come to that understanding about the reality of our being, then we miss the point of Jesus' teachings and his awakening gesture.

Insight 78

Jesus said, "Why have you come out into the desert?
To see a reed shaken by the wind? And to see a man
clothed in fine garments like your kings and your
great men? Upon them are the fine garments,
and they are unable to discern the truth."

From the Head ...

Again, this insight has a dual meaning. The obvious meaning is that wealthy, powerful people, those clothed in "fine garments," are caught up in their money and influence, and have no thirst for a larger reality. They are comfortable where they are, and are unable to see truth. This is consistent with Jesus' support of the poor.

On a much deeper level, however, this insight stabs at the heart of the Spirit having fallen into the world, and becoming comfortable with its sleep. It parallels Insights 28 and 29 where Jesus remarks that the Spirit has become "intoxicated," and he is "amazed at how this great wealth has made its home in this poverty." Which points out the irony: what we see as wealth in this world, is in actuality a "great poverty." So, those who are rich with this world, are poor in the other, and vice versa. The world in this insight is symbolized by the "desert." It is important for those who are awakening to come to terms with why they find themselves in this desolation.

Also a key point is that the "kings" and "great men" of this world, represent the dark spiritual forces that keep people trapped within the confines of this "desert." The word "garment" is an often used as a metaphor for physical reality. So, this insight makes it clear to the

187

spiritually awakened not to become enamored of these "powers" since they are unable to discern the truth.

From the Heart ...

"Why have you come out into the desert?" Jesus asks. I asked myself that same question on the many treks into the desert that I have made. What did I think I would find there? The answer was "nothing," of course. The desert represents to me the vast nothingness of the world system, even as it was beautiful and amazing in so many ways. I find that in the desert areas, I am pulled within myself. The heat, the barrenness of the terrain (yes, I know it is beautiful and full of "life") and the brutality of the ecosystem, all work to lay me bare somehow.

But precisely so, the desert in its own way, teaches me that all the clothing of the world is but a shadow of a world beyond it, that shines inside of me without failing, and points to a home that I long for. "Why have you come out into the desert?" Jesus asks. "To find my way," is the only answer I can muster.

Insight 79

A women from the crowd said to him, "Blessed are the womb which bore you and the breasts which nourished you." He said to her, "Blessed are those who have heard the word of the father and mother of light and have truly kept it. For there will be days when you will say, 'Blessed are the womb which has not conceived and the breasts which have not given milk.'"

From the Head ...

People seem to have an unconscious need to procreate, which we generally deem a good thing, since survival of the species depends on it. However, it is not necessarily a good thing individually, and can be quite harmful to our sense of being, and tie us up into an externalized pattern of behavior (child rearing and family life) in which our inner self becomes all the more lost.

Thomas is relaying this insight here, which also appears in the public Gospels, because it drives to the core of Jesus' private teachings as well. We seek meaning and purpose in our children and thereby in some future reality to come in the world, but that perspective is barren and without merit, Jesus is saying. The only essential reality that is needed is internal, and has nothing to do with what we have done or have not done external to that inner truth. In other more philosophical words, authentic being is not a historical activity, but a transcendental knowledge of self.

To say, as Jesus does here, that there will come a day when you say, "Blessed are the womb which has not conceived and the breasts which have not given milk," is to say, that there will come a time when all that you have once thought was important and sacred will vanish, and you will be left with nothing on the outside to hold on to. Anyone who has gone through a spiritual awakening knows the truth of this. Our children, our families, our things, our jobs, our political stature and power, as well as our economic strength – all these things are secondary realities, and pale into insignificance when examined in light of the larger spiritual reality. This is a core teaching for Jesus, as hard and harsh as it may first appear, and it is the most liberating reality there is.

From the Heart ...

Having a child as I do makes me ponder the essence of this insight a bit more than someone who doesn't. Yes, there have been times when I thought, "I would have been better off not having birthed a child – it only keeps me pinned down and less mobile." However, that is not how I always feel, and for the most part I value my son very much – not only as a son, but as a spiritual guide and an avenue of learning. But that is not what this insight is truly about.

It is easy to make our children, as well as our jobs or whatever else, the center of our lives, and create an identity for ourselves out of that center. If we do that, which most of us do, we only wrap ourselves deeper into the darkness of the world system. We can even, as we do, call this identity centering in the external "good." We deem it "spiritual" to be a "good" person in the world, "being responsible" and a "good citizen." But it is all a lie. The "goodness" that we think we take onto ourselves, only makes us participate in the essential darkness of the world all the more. The "good" that we will, is over matched by the dark context in which the "good" is done. If we are left with salvation or spirituality being merely "goodness" then we are hopeless for sure, since it is an impossible state of affairs in this dark context. Jesus himself denied being "good," not because he wasn't doing "good" things, but because he saw the question from a deeper point of view as a question about context, not behavior.

I have given up thinking in terms of good and evil, at least in the conventional sense. Nietzsche counseled that over a hundred years ago in his book: *Beyond Good and Evil*. He was right. Everything that is of true importance is done beyond the idea of good and evil. I think that is what Jesus is teaching here. It's a hard one, of course, because the world would rather you not see it. That is how control is maintained. To awaken places you beyond the primary control mechanisms of guilt, shame and the ideas of good and evil. We are not free until we take our freedom.

Insight 80

> *Jesus said, "He who has recognized the world has found the body, but he who has found the body is superior to the world."*

From the Head ...

This insight is basically a restatement of Insight 56. It is restated because it is central to understanding the teachings of Jesus. Many scholars, when reading this kind of Gospel statement, tend to place them in the realm of Christian lore, or later Gnostic thinking. I suspect, however, that Jesus said things like this to his companions – particularly in private, where they could be discussed at length.

In Insight 56 Jesus calls the world a "corpse," and here he refers to the world as the "body." Recognizing and finding the "body" as a "corpse" is critical to detaching from the power and ultimacy of physical reality. That is to say, it is central to awakening to see the world as not the core organizing principle of truth. This has long been a sore point in religion, and a basic conflict between Eastern and Western thought on the matter. In these insights, Jesus is much more Eastern in his understanding – finding that essential truth is internal not historical, and not a matter of material process.

From the Heart ...

The issue of physicality and material process as essentially important to spirituality has been overcome in me. I no longer think in those terms, and it has created a distance between how I view the world, and how the world is viewed in general by most folks. I have been accused, as I am sure Jesus was, as being a "world hater." I prefer to see myself as a "Spirit lover" instead. It is not so much that I "hate" the world as such, but rather I feel that physical process is separate from spiritual process. I feel a deep sense of what Jesus termed, "being in the world, but not of the world." To love life means to me to love beauty, tenderness and compassion – not the brutality of natural selection. It means being fully conscious and mindful – not lost in the blind process of existence. If that makes me a "world hater" then I guess I am, but I don't think of it in those terms. Not anymore. I have found the body, but I'm more than that.

Insight 81

> *Jesus said, "Let him who has grown rich be king,*
> *and let him who possesses power renounce it."*

From the Head ...

This insight appears to be a paradox at first reading. The first half suggests a condoning of wealth, while the second half denounces it. However, like most of these private and secret insights, we have to go beyond the surface words for the true meaning.

Let us read this insight this way: "Let him who knows himself understand his true royalty, and let him who has become powerful in the world renounce it." I write it this way, because that is what makes sense in the context of these teachings. "Power" in the world is like being rich with a false reality. To renounce it is to renounce the falseness of its meaning and influence. Remember, for Jesus the Spirit is regal and ultimate – it is royal. The world is empty, a "corpse" that is not "worthy" of the ultimate.

This insight must be read exactly as it is placed in this listing by Thomas. Although it is separated, it is a natural and logical conclusion to the previous saying. Jesus' focus is always to lead people away from their fixation and immersion in the world. This insight makes most sense read that way.

From the Head ...

The ancient Gnostics were accused by the orthodox church "fathers" of being "elitists." That, of course, was far from the truth, as many of their pronouncements were. The Gnostics were not ones to be controlled easily, since they followed inner wisdom and not external doctrine or church law. They literally took themselves, their True Self that is, to be princely and royal – something that should be valued above all else and never to be submitted to any earthly authority. This "princely" knowledge was essential to spiritual enlightenment, and while it did make a distinction between those who "knew" and those who didn't, it was not meant as an accusation against those who were struggling in the world to find themselves.

I never think of myself as being beyond people, or better than everyone else. Those are concepts that the world fosters, and not the Spirit. There are those who know themselves and those who don't. That is just an observation, and not an indictment. Those who don't know who they are are, are not less valuable because they don't know it. While it makes me a bit sad to see those who are royal treat themselves as if they are slaves, I look past all the delusional powers to see who they are, and try to stay very clear about that in the way I walk through the world. "Treat others as you would be treated," is a teaching of Jesus that applies. We commonly call it the "golden rule," and so it is – for Spirit reasons, not earthly ones.

Insight 82

> Jesus said, "He who is near me is near the fire,
> and he who is far from me is far from the kingdom."

From the Head ...

Fire, as is water, is often a metaphor for Spirit. The Spirit is ablaze in the teachings of Jesus, and anyone who comes near cannot but be affected by them. Like a fire that burns out of control, the spiritual "fire" is dangerous to those who wish to find a sense of comfort in the world. It burns you up, and makes ashes of the material system. It destroys the false reality of the world.

Fire also purifies. To be near the fire is to have all the impurities of the world melted away, impurities such as unconsciousness of being, intoxication with the world, and ignorance of the Spirit. Being conscious, aware, awake and tuned in, is being near the kingdom.

From the Heart ...

I love fireplaces. On a cold wintry day, to sit by the fire is pure luxury and beauty. I always find myself staring into the flames, as if something in those ever-changing darts of fire are going to speak something to me that I dare not miss.

Most of us are fascinated by fire. It means warmth and shelter. It also means survival and power. Without fire, we're in big trouble physically. We use it to heat our water, cook our food, and sometimes to light our way. Without fire, the night would be dark indeed. This was more true for the ancient mind set than ours, but I think it is still somewhat true.

Many of our symbols are based on fire. The burning bush of Moses, the flame of Pentecost for Christians, and the candlelight symbolizing knowledge, or romance. When we are closest to our symbols, we are closest to something transcendent in us – something beyond the darkness that is dispelled by the fire. Even "building" a fire has a ritualistic feel to it, whether one is camping or staying home on a long winter night. It is spiritual, and has been seen as such from the beginning.

Helping someone awaken is like "building a fire under them," although to be more accurate, we should say it is like setting their fire free. It doesn't surprise me that Jesus would use the symbol of fire as a symbol for the Spirit. He didn't begin this tradition or idea, but he makes good use of it.

In the Gnostic Gospel of Philip, written much later, Philip likens the world to winter – cold and bitter. Without fire, ancient man would have died. It is no coincidence that the Gnostics used the word "spark" interchangeably with Spirit, for without the Spirit we are nothing but "corpses."

I like to think of my Spirit as a "spark" of the divine. The imagery feels warm and satisfying, like sitting next to the fire on a cold night. It's romantic, appealing and life-giving. It helps me get through the world, which is what I think Jesus was getting at in this insight.

Insight 83

> Jesus said, "Images are visible to people,
> but the light within them remains hidden in the
> image of the Father's light. He will be disclosed,
> but his image will remain hidden by his light."

From the Head ...

This insight is rather esoteric in nature. It reflects, I think, Jesus' intellectual depth of understanding. The language of this insight suggests that Jesus was influenced by Plato's philosophy, which should not surprise us, since Plato was perhaps the most dominate philosophical force of that time, and one of the most insightful thinkers ever to live. The use of philosophical language by Jesus has had scholars in debate for years, with many of them thinking that word usage like this could not be authentic Jesus language, since he did not typically speak in such a way. Of course, we have to ask: how do they know that? Their answer comes from available public literature, which, as we know, was doctored by orthodox thinkers who perhaps filtered out anything they deemed too unconventional. So, I think we should treat this insight as it appears here – from the mouth of Jesus.

The idea here is a rather complex one. Jesus makes a distinction between image and what is visible – alluding to the nature of spirituality itself. That which is "visible" has less spiritual significance than that which is underneath it. The "image" of something precedes its visibility, like a seed contains the genetic coding of the visible structure of a plant before that plant grows. But in this insight Jesus is reminding us not to confuse the visible world of things with the hidden reality beyond them. This is well in keeping with his position in these private instructions.

For Jesus, as for Gnostic Christians after him, the world came into being in a flawed manner, and does not reflect the fullness of the spiritual order. It is, in a sense, pre-mature and incomplete. The construction of the world was brought about by a secondary aspect of the divine world called a demiurge, which insufficiently ordered the created cosmos from a shadow of something it didn't understand. Which is why, Jesus suggests in these insights, we feel the emptiness and longing that we do. It is the nature of this created world, not some behavioral, moral or psychological fault of ours.

To see the truth, one has to see under the visible forms to the inner image. The father's light rest within, not on the surface of things. To attempt to prove the existence of God from the vastness of the material matrix of the cosmos is sheer foolishness, Jesus would assert. The God of light is mysterious, not in the process of "things," nor merely in the center of the stuff of the universe. God is the "image" beyond, and within. This point, Jesus felt, was important to make in many different ways, so people would not get lost in the shadow play of the world.

From the Heart ...

Carlos Castaneda revealed the art of "seeing," as taught to him by Don Juan Matus - a self-described sorcerer. "Seeing" was a perceptual change from the ordinary way in which we view the world. It is seeing a reality within visible forms that we commonly overlook. Like seeing the energy of a thing, instead of the form of a thing. To "see" requires a re-adjustment of reality orientation.

When I first read Castaneda's books, I was a bit overwhelmed and even a little frightened, I have to admit. This was many years ago, and I lived on the surface of the world at that time, and even my reading of these books was a stretch. They changed my life, for once I begin to think that something else was happening that I couldn't normally see,

I was motivated to start the journey into actually acquiring the knowledge needed to "see" the world as Castaneda suggested. I feel that same way every time I read these insights from Jesus.

To look for the "light within" is a remarkable way of living. After all, life really is boring without the mystery of that which is beyond it. Physical being is just a set of clearly moving objects, doing that which is by and large predictable. But the world of light beyond! That has no predictability to it, and reveals itself like a hide and go seek game.

Most of us are simply stuck. That is the best way of putting it. We are stuck with the reality that we have learned, and don't have a clue as to how to get free, particularly since we don't even see that we are stuck.

All this leads me to admit to myself that spirituality has been a life long process of learning how to express it, even as I was experiencing it. I still feel uneasy with it, because I know that all my words are deficient, and only visible forms of something that is hidden underneath. It is the way it is.

Insight 84

Jesus said, "When you see your likeness, you rejoice. But when you see your image which came into being before you, and which neither dies nor become visible, how much you will have to bear!"

From the Head ...

In Gnostic thinking each person has a heavenly twin who awaits our return. At death, if one knows the way through the labyrinth of the world, they can be re-united. Perhaps this idea derives from Jesus himself, although it is not spoken of often in his teachings. But this insight seems more to relate to awakening itself.

For Jesus, awakening was a kind of rebirth, an acknowledgment of an inner reality that does not die, nor has its origin in this world. To awaken is to become aware of your own Spirit. You discover that you and the divine are of one substance – Spirit, and as a Spirit you resides in a wasteland of lost tears – the suffering of this world. The idea of awakening Jesus also called an "un-timely birth" (The Gospel of John), because upon awakening a Spirit is thrust into its dilemma of lostness. It is not a pleasant thing, but necessary.

Here Jesus says that awakening is "much ... to bear." It shocks the system, so to speak, and jars everything we thought we knew. We go through life thinking we know who we are, but the truth is we don't have the slightest idea, until that occurrence of awakening knocks us off our feet into the pit of our real situation.

Jesus never soft soaped this idea. He, as always, just lays it out plainly and in straightforward language. When you see your Spirit, it will shake you to the roots, he is saying.

From the Heart ...

Jesus wasn't kidding. To see your own Spirit is an event of unprecedented disturbance in your life. It is, as this insight suggests, "much ... to bear." I still feel the aftershocks of having awakened. It ripples through my life like a giant thunderstorm or earthquake. When I read apocalyptic literature about the "end times," I understand these sayings to exist in me currently – not as some external historical event to happen to the world, but to each of us upon awakening.

An insight like this cannot mean much to a person who reads it merely from the intellect. I did that for years, and although I thought it brilliant and meaningful, it didn't impact me the way it does now upon awakening to its truth in a real way. Everything changes, and you cannot return to a state of total ignorance again. It requires much of you to bear, for upon knowing this deep truth, you cannot let it be unspoken.

Such is the power of the Spirit when stirred. Your soul is disturbed and looks inward to a vastness never explored, and becomes alive with the presence of something it could not have devised of its own accord. Quite literally the world becomes a kind of nothingness from which your release is always imminent. And, your task becomes simple – stir the waters of the world until the Spirit moves having shaken off its sleep. Your old friends won't like that much, and think you've gone mad. Your family may disown you, thinking you've joined a religious cult of some kind. But there are those who know – and that makes a difference. To become a friend of the Spirit is to become detached from the world.

Insight 85

Jesus said, "Adam came into being from a great power and a great wealth, but he did not become worthy of you. For had he been worthy, he would not have experienced death."

From the Head ...

Adam, as the first man, was given a place of honor in Jewish theology of the time. In the early Christian church much was made of Jesus being the "second Adam" – or new man. However, in this insight Jesus is making reference to Adam not being "worthy" of those to whom he is speaking. It is clear that he is talking about the Spirit that has become awakened in those that he is teaching.

The metaphor here is that Adam represents that part of us that is created by the forces and powers of the world. In Gnostic thinking this part was the soul, or psyche – which was the origin of all mental and emotional attributes. It is the "Adam" of each of our beings. The Spirit, however, is something that was not fashioned by this world's creator. It is an alien to this world – a kind of separate reality the defies definition by earthly language. It is the "Eve" in us.

In this insight it appears that Jesus is speaking directly to the Spirit. The tie between "Adam and Eve," the soul and Spirit, is important, for it is the soul part of us that moves in this world and either becomes merely a function of material existence, or an agent of the Spirit. It is not worthy of the Spirit, in that it does not have the same origin as the Spirit. The soul dies, since it is a part of this world – a world where death rules. The Spirit is immortal, and has as its place of origin a world of light where death is not a reality.

This distinction is important, since it drives to the heart of the complex nature of our existence here, and the entrapment of the Spirit that is so central to Jesus' teachings. Our Spirit is not made up of the mental and emotional features we tend to identify as being who we are. These features, however, can be used by the Spirit as a force of liberation, or can be used by the world as a force of enslavement. Perhaps this is where all the stories of "selling one's soul to the devil" come from originally. The soul is the pivotal part of wakening that either aids the Spirit through the world, or submerges it into unconscious intoxicating sleep.

From the Heart ...

Each of us struggles with our emotional and mental make up. All the issues of our psychological self exist within that make up, and it is something that we generally identify as being who we are. This is why we get so caught up in all the emotionality of life, and wrap our thinking around feelings and psychological factors that keep us locked into patterns. We "believe" this is who we are, and all the information generated by our actions in the world are validations of this "truth."

However, this is not who we are as spiritual beings. Our Spirit is not our mental and emotional features, and has a reality to it that defies definition and description, although we try. I look at the situation between the soul and Spirit like this: the soul can either draw its reality from looking out (the world) or by looking in (the Spirit). The soul is that function that activates the reality. If the soul looks outward for its reality base, we become part of the world in everything we do. In a sense, we lose our souls to the world. If our soul is turned inward and derives its source of truth from the Spirit, it becomes an agent of that Spirit, and walks through the world enlightened, and becomes part and parcel of the Spirit. The soul, therefore, is sometimes referred to as "the twin" – since it looks like the Spirit, but is not the same as the Spirit, nor does it have the same source.

In some metaphysical thinking on this subject, the soul – which is our earthly identity, can become so identified with the Spirit as to accompany the Spirit out of this world upon death. Personal identity is therefore maintained, but spiritual wholeness is also achieved. Kind of like having your cake and eating it too. Without this identification, the soul is dissolved by the force and powers of the world, which literally feed upon it as a source of energy and fuel. The unawakened Spirit is swept into the pattern of the world once again, and "re-grows" another soul. This process reoccurs until the soul and Spirit move out of the world force by deliberate act of spiritual will.

I have found that the above description best fits what I see happening in the world. It is not a pleasant sight, but the harshness of material reality never is. This harshness is one of the fundamental reasons why people stay asleep, and seek to deny the truth of their being. Although their denial keeps them locked into the terror, they don't see it – which is their immediate goal, and they become unwitting slaves to it's system.

It was not easy for me to come to this conclusion, and it took a great deal of inner work and contemplation to break free from my own denial. Gnosis is hard work, but the outcome is one of pure awe.

Insight 86

> *Jesus said, "The foxes have their holes and the birds have their nests, but the son of man has no place to lay his head and rest."*

From the Head ...

The son of man refers, once again, to the Spirit. In Gnostic circles, which make direct claim to Jesus' private teachings, the true God of Light is named Man, which is why Jesus referred to his spiritual self as "the son of man." This spiritual reality has no real place in this world. It is an alien, and in a sense homeless – a stranger in a strange land.

Jesus is not suggesting, as some scholars have thought, a nomadic lifestyle. It is not necessary, since the Spirit is Jesus' concern, and it already is nomadic and without place in the world. This insight, therefore, is a simple statement of spiritual reality – not a lifestyle recommendation.

From the Heart ...

Even though I see these kinds of insights as statements of truth regarding the nature of spiritual being in the world, and not lifestyle recommendations, I find myself becoming a bit more nomadic nevertheless. The link between how we identify ourselves and our lifestyle is a valid point to be made. The more I have detached from the world as a defining power, the more I find myself not wanting to be too locked in anywhere. That is not to say I do not find a residence satisfying and important – I do. One may live well, and still be rather unattached.

However, it is easy to slip into the pattern of identifying oneself with where one lives. I think that is the critical factor that I had to come to terms with. It is more an inner reality check than anything I do on the outside by way of behavior or activity. Yet, I feel that this inner reality check is important as a daily thing. This insight can be used as a prayer of reminder I think, and I have done so on occasion. It helped, and so I use it from time to time.

Insight 87

> Jesus said, "Wretched is the body that is
> dependent upon a body, and wretched is the
> soul that is dependent on these two."

From the Head ...

Every creature depends on the death of other creatures to live. That is the material system – the food chain. It is impossible to escape this system while remaining in it. Even those who have become vegetarians participate in this system. It is, as it is often referred to, a fact of life. What we call a life system, from another perspective is a death system, since the two are locked together in a physical mechanism of reality.

Here Jesus refer to this system as "wretched." Being dependent on the death of other creatures to maintain one's life is spiritually abhorrent. It is deficient and in error, according to Jesus. When the soul becomes identified with this process of death, instead of turning to the Spirit for its life, it is truly "wretched" indeed. But this is precisely the situation of the majority of "souls" existing in the world. They become part of the process instead of turning away and detaching from the world, and then allying itself to the Spirit.

This situation of the soul has prompted many to speak of it as a warfare or battleground. The soul is literally pulled in two directions, and cannot stay neutral. Either the soul becomes an ally of the Spirit or the world. There is no "peace" between the two, as Jesus refers to in many of his teachings. This situation is "wretched," Jesus admits, but it is of critical importance to recognize the situation as it is, without glossing over its harshness or brutality. Thus it remains a core principle in these insights.

From the Heart ...

I was having coffee one morning out on my patio. As I sat there sipping my java, I watched a cricket as it hopped toward the bushes. In a flash, a lizard darted out of the plants and snatched the cricket in its jaws, and ran back to the bushes, having gotten a "good breakfast" for itself. I just went on drinking my coffee.

I thought about this insignificant incident on my patio, and how I was literally unfazed by its "wretchedness." Life maintained in the jaws of death, and all life plotted out by the power of death. What a strange reality, I thought later. The cricket was "guilty" of exposing himself. The penalty – loss of life.

I saw that we, too, are a part of this "wretched" process, and that we spend our time trying not to expose ourselves to forces that can "eat" us, but in the end, we cannot live without that exposure. What a tragic state of affairs! We can call this process good, but we cease to call it good when it is we, or our child, that is exposed to a man-eating virus, or a speeding car, or whatever deathtrap awaits. Our romantic mind trick wanes then. How unconscious we are. How oblivious to the wretchedness of the world we become. Yes, it is awesome and vast. Yes, it is beautiful and wondrous, but it is not a good place at all – dangerous and deadly. Until we get that, we never loosen from its grip, and turn toward something more – a spiritual reality that is beyond all the "wretched" process of existence. It took me a long time to get it, but I get it now.

Insight 88

> Jesus said, "The angels and the
> prophets will come to you and give to
> you things you already have. And you, too,
> give them those things which you have,
> and say to yourselves, 'When will they
> come and take what is theirs?'"

From the Head ...

"The angels and prophets will come to you and give to you things you already have" – that is how the opening of this insight reads. It is like saying "they give you more of the same." For Jesus, and the true spiritual community, the angels and prophets are agents of this world; voices that speak of things here, but have no reference to the world of light from which the Spirit originates. And, to be sure, if you read most of what is said by the prophets of Israel and the messages of the angels, what you come up with is a lot of talk about this world, and what activity here will make it better. For Jesus, that is not spirituality at all, but just "things you already have."

When we make a religion out of these "things that we already have," we become all the more lost in a maze of attempts to make the world become what it can never become. In Insight 93 Jesus will say, "Do not throw the pearls to swine," a reference to not giving your soul to the world. He leads up to that teaching here, by basically saying not to give the angels and the prophets a hearing. We cannot forget that for Jesus, these angels and prophets are part of a "wretched" system that seeks to keep the Spirit trapped in its darkness by deception and illusion.

From the Heart . . .

There was a time when I was very involved in political activity, thinking that I could "change the world." That idealistic sentiment is shared by the majority of people who believe that if we could just somehow all become nicer and more loving toward one another, our world would become a heaven on earth. That is a false and erroneous claim. Because of the hardened processes of the world, and the material matrix in which we are fixed, no amount of love or moral righteousness can change the basis flaw within the process.

Most people will not want to hear that, and they will suggest that I am being cynical and negative; too dark. But that is not true. The basic processes are unaffected by our activity and our beliefs. While it is true that our love for one another is the only path that makes sense, and does in fact make our lives more comfortable and joyous, those things do not change the basic brutality of the world. Viruses would still kill children, accidents would still happen, and everything and everybody would still die as a matter of course. Even if we were all morally perfect and totally loving, the world would still hurt. It would still maintain its basic darkness.

All this is to say that the world is dark – that is its nature. All my wanting it to be different will not make it so. I can chose to act differently, more consciously and lovingly, but I will still be "forced" to participate on some level in a dark system that I wish to overcome. We have to eat and breath – and walk through the world. Every time we take a step we kill creatures. Every time we eat, we contribute to the death system, and every time we try to manage and protect ourselves from the accidents and flaws in life, our actions leave us vulnerable elsewhere. That is the way it is, like it or not.

So, any religion that has as its cornerstone an accusation that human beings are the cause of all the suffering and pain in the world are just more of the same old talk – like angels and prophets who "give us what we already have."

Spiritual truth is about a separate reality that has as its basic core something that cannot be found in the natural course of this world. It is so far beyond its scope and reality as to be rendered impossible by the voices of this world. But impossible it is not! There is a higher reality beyond this material matrix. It was before anything material existed, and will be long after the physical universe has vanished. That is what Jesus is teaching here in this insight.

Insight 89

*Jesus said, "Why do you wash the outside of the cup?
Do you not realize that he who made the inside
is the same one who made the outside?"*

From the Head ...

The outside is like the inside, this insight suggests. The best way to understand this is to simply see that our psychological self and our behavioral self are intermixed, and are made together out of the stuff of the world. This is in keeping with later Gnostic thinking that human beings are composed of three elements, two of which are of the same basic source. The material, the psychic – which have this world as its origin – and the Spirit, which has as its source a "world of light" that is a separate reality altogether. Often times we confuse our psychological self with our spiritual self, and on this point Jesus is teaching in this insight.

Another point that can be made here is that to change our way of living, we also have to change our way of thinking. We can "wash" the outside all we want, but nothing will change in our lives until our basic reality focus changes.

Like most of Jesus' insights, dual meanings are available. They can be viewed from many different angles, each having a power and force for enlightenment. This insight is clearly one of those instances where psychological development and spiritual realization go hand in hand.

From the Heart ...

As I wrote about this insight, I began to feel myself tense up. I was reacting to times when I was told to "straighten up" or "get my act together." Conforming to established norms of behavior is like "washing the outside of the cup" without realizing that the inside of us is made of the same conformity. How interested we are in making everyone "toe the mark" and fit in. There is a great deal of social consensual pressure to create a certain reality.

This reality pressure starts from the first moment of birth, and continues until death. It takes a great deal of courage and strength to pull away, and seek truth more authentically. When I read an insight like this one, which seems so easy on its surface, I become aware of how difficult it is in actuality. It is like seeing that my psychological self is just as controlled as my external behavior, and the two are linked together by a social consensual matrix that is immense in its length and breadth in my life. To truly loosen the grip, I have to wash both inside and outside of my "cup." Once again I am aware of how hard the work is.

Insight 90

Jesus said, "Come unto me, for my yoke is easy and my lordship is mild, and you will find repose for yourselves."

From the Head ...

Most religious understandings in the western world are blame based notions about human beings. We tend to take on to ourselves responsibility for death, disease and decay. Little wonder that we feel as we do about ourselves – not too good, by most accounts. What Jesus is doing in this insight is a re-framing of how we think. He says, in essence, that authentic awakening goes easy on self blame, and therefore is an easy "yoke." He is not saying that awakening itself is easy.

The word repose is a word Gnostics used to express spiritual centering. A person who has come to the truth of his/her being has reached "repose," a kind of inner serenity that is immovable by external force. Perhaps they used the word because Jesus used it in reference to this inner aspect of self knowledge.

It is important to link the idea of easy yoke with repose in this insight. Self-knowledge brings about an easiness in one's life, since the inner conflict developed and fostered by the world is overcome. We literally can rest with who we are, and not be fraught with the turmoil of constructing ourselves daily in the world of functional life – which is what the social consensual world does.

"Come unto me" is an invitation to come to the Spirit. It is not meant as a invitation to worship Jesus, or to set him up as something apart from what and who we ourselves are. This insight is a beautiful and tender announcement of our own spiritual inner truth, one that releases us from the bondage of all else, and frees us to be the divine reality that we each hold inside.

From the Heart ...

Don Juan taught Carlos Castaneda that we could either make ourselves strong, or make ourselves miserable – the amount of energy it takes is the same. I found that to be true. Most people work very hard at being miserable, although they are unaware of how hard they are working at it. To be strong, like being miserable, requires energy – but directed differently. It's all an "inside job," as one of my AA friends once put it.

Without realizing it, I spent most of my life trying to "fix" myself through external means. For a time my effort would pay off, but then it would collapse like a house of cards. I was spending massive amounts of energy on externalized notions of myself, and it wasn't until utter exhaustion led me to giving up the battle for happiness, that I began the journey inside myself and gained "repose."

The idea of happiness has a kind of edge to it. As a therapist people would come to me and say, "I'm not happy." I would ask them, "What does that mean – to be happy?" I discovered they could never really put a final definition to it, which was why they could never actually achieve it. Happiness was a feeling that they could not hang on to, although they felt as if they should be able to through some relational or objective magic. They were miserable. My first task was to get them to give up on their clutching, so that happiness as a fleeting feeling could be enjoyed again.

Once awakened the Spirit does not clutch onto people, places or things. It does not hold onto forms that trap it. I think that is what Jesus was driving at in this insight. To come to the Spirit is to release our grip on everything else. It is easier, and it leads to the serenity of authentic self-knowledge.

Insight 91

They said to him, "Tell us who you are so that we may believe in you." He said to them, "You read the face of the sky and of the earth, but you have not recognized the one who is before you, and you do not know how to read this moment."

From the Head ...

It is easy for us to know the things of the world. Our mind is geared for such things. But to know the Spirit? That is something that must reveal itself, since we have no idea where to look, or what we would be looking at if we saw it. This insight, like many in this collection, is written from the perspective of the Spirit. To make this a literal question to Jesus would be to diminish its value. That, of course, is how most scholars and lay people have read a saying like this, but then the more essential truth is missed.

"You have not come to recognize the one who is before you (or in your presence)," is the key to this insight – for what is in our presence, or "before" us, as this teaching has it, is something alien to the "face of the sky and of the earth." It is not recognizable except through a re-orientation of the soul and an awakening of the Spirit. Earlier Jesus taught that he was revealing "what no eye has ever seen, no ear ever heard" (Insight 17). This insight is connected to that teaching, for it reinforces the difficulty faced by those willing to do the work of the Spirit. We know a great deal about the world, but we know nothing of the Spirit, for the world has shielded its presence from us, and kept us in the dark. We don't even recognize the moment of our awakening, until after the fact.

This insight has a cutting edge to it if read from this mystical point of view. It is not a teaching about Jesus' personhood, but rather an insight about who we are, and why we can't see what is before us.

From the Heart ...

I was reading a magazine article about alien abductions recently. To be honest, I don't place much stock in these reports. Maybe yes, maybe no. In the final analysis, extraterrestrial life doesn't change much, except that there are other life forms caught in the same dilemma that we are – whether they are more highly technological is beside the point. But I was struck that in each of these cases the individuals were struggling to define the indefinable for them. They had an experience that they could not place into any known category, except a technological, extraterrestrial framework. They could "read the signs of the earth and sky," but "could not recognize what was before them."

Perhaps our modern day fascination with flying saucers, space aliens and abductions, has more to do with our encounters with something inside of us that we cannot come to terms with, than it does with actual invaders from across the vast reaches of space. And so, we simply define this experience in the way we are able.

At any rate, spiritual experience is not easily categorized and defined. We can't just slap a label on it and make it fit neatly into our pre-packed reality. It disturbs us and abducts us from our sense of the world. It probes us without mercy, and we feel that we have had something implanted in us that won't let us go. That is the nature of spiritual experience – it is beyond us, and yet right on top of us. That is the way it has always felt to me. I never recognized it until after it was gone.

Insight 92

*Jesus said, "Seek and you will find.
Yet, what you asked me about in former
times and which I did not tell you then
now I do desire to tell, but you
do not inquire after it."*

From the Head ...

There is a time and place for everything. We often desire to know something before we can understand it, and then when we are able to comprehend, we don't ask. When we are children we are curious and explorative, but then we grow dense and rigid. We cease to ask after the truth of something, because we have already made up our minds. We literally stop searching. In other teachings Jesus spoke of "becoming like children." This is what he was getting at.

Imagine the world as a labyrinth. It has many twists and turns, and is very confusing. If we were to sit in one place refusing to move, our ability to find our way out would literally be stopped by our ceasing to search. If, on the other hand, we continue our search in an exhaustive manner, then we could find our way. "Seek and you will find," but are we truly seeking? Or, have we already made up our minds, and merely created a self validating circle of logic that keeps us trapped?

Jesus was rather hard on folks who claimed religious superiority, and yet maintained only the illusion of spiritual insight. It's important to keep our minds unattached from rigid thought patterns that destroy our ability to "seek and find."

219

From the Heart ...

Most of us have a very narrow pattern of reality behavior in our lives. We ritualistically sustain and maintain our reality through constant agreement with the pattern. We may say that we are seeking spirituality, but what we are really doing is simply trying to discover a meaningfulness to our already pre-set reality pattern.

Authentic spirituality requires disruption to our reality patterns and agreements. To seek, we have to detach from our everyday rituals, and allow ourselves the fluidity of something else to occur.

Whenever I make a statement like that, I always get asked: "How do I do that?" Well, the truth is, it has more to do with "not doing" as Don Juan taught Carlos Castaneda, than it does with doing something. In other words, it has to do with suspending what you would ordinarily do, and not replacing it with another activity. That is not the same as just sitting there waiting for something to happen. It is allowing reality to be fluid and alive and accepting presentation of something unfamiliar. After all, if we are honest, we seek the familiar in our lives, because it is comfortable, although perhaps not easy.

It is our tendency to fix on patterns and remain locked into those patterns. We stop "inquiring" or "seeking." For me it has helped to simply ask myself, "Am I open?" If I am not, I can then make that change inside of myself by simply denying the patterns their power. Most spiritual work is asking the right question. When we do, the answers seek us.

Insight 93

Jesus said, "Do not give what is holy to dogs, lest they throw them on the dung heap. Do not throw the pearls to swine, lest they (devour them)."

From the Head ...

This insight also appears in the public Gospels, and has a great deal of practical appeal to it. It makes sense to not give something to someone or something that they cannot understand or appreciate. Like giving a very valuable watch to a small child, who would probably break it in no time. The responsibility would be on the giver, who made a poor judgment as to the ability of the recipient.

"Do not throw the pearls to swine." Recall that "pearl" is often used as a metaphor for the Spirit, and thus this insight suggest that we make very clear judgments as to whom we share our spiritual self with. The last two words in this insight have been obscured, so the words "devour them" are mine. I felt that was in keeping with the general thrust of this insight, and Jesus' teachings in this collection.

From the Heart ...

There is an old joke that goes: Don't try to teach a pig to sing, it costs a lot of money, and makes the pig mad. I think that joke is a most accurate addendum to this insight. I have found that spiritual revelation given to those who cannot appreciate it or understand it at all, generally become enraged. This insight is very much like a person who tells a secret to someone who they know will tell it to everyone else. Who is the fool? The person who told the secret, or the person who was just being who they are? The first, of course. Don't be foolish with your spirituality. Know when to walk away, and when to keep your mouth shut. Don't argue with "swine." It will just make them angry, and you will never convince them anyway.

In the public Gospels, Jesus is said to have gone to church only one time, and had a bad experience there. They literally wanted to stone him. On the other hand, those same texts tell us, that "tax collectors, drunks and prostitutes" were quite willing to hear something different. "Swine" can look very neat and clean, and accurate recipients of spiritual revelation can be unwashed and poor. Be careful! Use your intuition and brains.

Insight 94

*Jesus said, "He who seeks will find,
and he who knocks will be let in."*

From the Head ...

This insight is grouped together with others like it. They all have
to do with our openness to authentic spiritual awakening. But this
saying, in a very simple way, says something a little more. If we are
open and authentic, and we do our work (knocking on the door), this
insight says, something on the other side of the "door" will let us in.
There is a power to the spiritual world that seeks us as well, and "lets
(us) in" when we "knock" upon it.

In later Gnostic thinking, the world as a closed system is literally
ringed by a limit, or wall. Within that wall is a doorway to the other
world, the world of light. To cross that limit or wall, one must knock on
the door, and allow it to be opened from the other side. We cannot open
it from this side. The intrigue here is that only an awakened Spirit knows
that this world is a closed off reality, and only the awakened Spirit
knows to go to the door and knock. Unawakened spirits are simply
swept back into the system unaware of what is truly happening to them.

An awakened Spirit seeks the limit, the wall around the universe. It
knocks and is answered by being opened from the other side. Awaiting
the Spirit there is a homecoming celebration. This insight, while short
and simple, packs a spiritual punch, if you read it from spiritual eyes.

From the Heart ...

Bob Dylan wrote a song titled: "Knocking on Heaven's Door."
Every time I hear it I think of this insight. We tend to think of the

universe as all reality. That the energy and matter that comprises the universality of all things, is all there is. Yes, that is a great deal. It is vast, but as we know now, it is not infinite, in that it had a beginning, and will come to an end. Knowing that is a kind of "knocking on heaven's door." Heaven, of course, is a metaphor for another reality beyond all known reality. "Heaven" is a reality outside of the universe of realities that frames physicality.

Can we experience that separate reality even while we are locked into the fold of this reality? The answer is yes, and no. The answer is yes, in that our spiritual True Self is a part of that other reality, and so by experiencing it, we experience that other world. The answer is no, in that our experience of our own Spirit is mixed with the experiences of this world, and only envisioned through the lens of our soul that sees only dimly, or as St. Paul put it: "through a glass darkly."

It is hard for modern and post-modern man to have a sense of "being other than" this world. We are educated and trained to think in certain ways, and those patterns of thought are extremely hard to break through. Even harder than it was almost 2,000 years ago in Jesus' time. Evolution, as a adaptive trait, is not a friend to spiritual consciousness. Human beings have adapted to this world more and more, and no longer even conceive of being something else apart from it. That there is a spiritual quality that defies definition and description outside of energy and matter will be objected to by rationalists inside both the field of science and religion as well. It is simply inconceivable that there is a third category that is dissimilar. That is why these "secret insights" are so radical and important.

Most "spiritual" books today confuse spirituality and soul making. They are not the same thing, as I have described elsewhere. Whenever energy is mentioned, you know that it no longer is a discussion of the Spirit. To experience the Spirit is to experience something that is not definable, nor can it be said to "exist" at all, since existence is a fashioning of energy and matter. So, I may know my spiritual True Self, but I talk around it, since I cannot genuinely talk about it. That is the difficulty of this work. And, that is why the "door" must be opened from the outside (or inside depending on your point of view), and we can only "knock" upon it.

Insight 95

Jesus said, "If you have money, do not lend it at interest but give it to one from whom you will not get it back."

From the Head ...

The primary thing that occurs when you get involved with "lending" money is that it involves you in the world with a spider web of connections. Money, arguably, is the cornerstone of all organized society, and as such it plays the most important role in all that the organized society does. Since the organized society is a kind of secondary reality that diverts attention from the spiritual dilemma, Jesus felt that it was dangerous for spiritually minded folks to get involved with it at all.

The intention of this insight is to, once again, maintain the focus onto matters that are critical to the Spirit. On this level Jesus is always consistent. To lend money with expectation of repayment is to create a psychological set of factors that foster anxiety, worry and external focus. If, on the other hand, you are not concerned with repayment, then the factors do not activate. Jesus is not saying, if you will notice, that spiritual people shouldn't have money, or even have enough money to give away. His primary concern is focus. What detracts from spiritual concentration is not worthy of doing. That is Jesus' point, as always.

From the Heart ...

I learned to worry about money from my Dad. He always worried. When we were on vacation, he was miserable because we were always "spending too much money." It wasn't that he didn't have enough. He had plenty. But, having grown up during the Depression, he was always concerned that it would somehow go away, and if that happened, his, and our, comfort would evaporate.

I learned this "worry" well. Even when I knew I had plenty, I was anxious that something would happen to destroy my comfort. I wasn't conscious of this situation, of course, but it was always there. Worry and anxiety. I think most people are like that. We are taught to worship money as a defense against the misfortunes and terror of life. We may rebel against the word "worship," but it is an accurate portrayal of how we honor the green stuff.

For example, it's not unusual for people to tell the most intimate of sexual details publicly. We seem to have broken that taboo. Ask someone about their sex life, and they probably will tell you. On the other hand, try asking someone how much they make, ah, then you find out what's really sacred. They will tell you in no uncertain language, "That's none of your business." Money is very personal, even if sex isn't anymore.

To look at our relationship with money is critical. Aside from all the "abundance preachers" out there, who teach worship of money with a smile on their face, instead of the hidden anxiety that is normal in society, money isn't questioned as to what it means and how we feel about it. For me it has been important just to look at my fear of not having money, and the lack of power and esteem that would be caused by such an event. What bogs me down? How does money worries change my focus, and push me away from spirituality? Good questions to ponder. Jesus was right on target with this issue, at least for the vast majority of us.

Insight 96

*Jesus said, "The kingdom of the father
(and mother) is like a certain woman. She took a
little leaven, concealed it in some dough, and made
it into large loaves. Let him who has ears hear."*

From the Head ...

Whenever Jesus ends an insight with the words, "Let him who has ears hear," you know that an esoteric meaning is also placed within the teaching. He is saying, in essence, pay attention beyond the obvious meaning. The common understanding of this insight is that the leaven is faith, and on a simplistic level that is true. Authentic spirituality begins with faith. But if spirituality stays simply a matter of "faith," it loses itself in authority issues, and never achieves the experience of self-knowledge – where faith is transcended. Faith, in this sense, is like a baby's first attempts at crawling. To remain at a crawl is to avoid taking the steps into full growth and authentic life. This was Jesus' objection to most religious understandings – they kept people at a crawl, so they could be controlled and manipulated by authority.

Then, this short parable has a very important esoteric message that is core to everything Jesus teaches: inside of us something is "concealed" that is more important than the "dough" that wraps around it, for without understanding that hidden quality, you cannot know truth.

In Gnostic thinking, the leaven of this parable is the Spirit that is placed in the "dough" of the creator's world without his specific understanding of it. It is hidden, not only from us who are the "dough" – elsewhere described as "the world corpse" or "the body"

– but also from the creator of the dough mixture, which in this case is the creator of the world itself.

The "error" of the creator God is that he thinks that his creation has life because he has made it so. But the real reason is that the Spirit gives it life, and since he does not understand the full nature of that Spirit, he does not understand the nature of reality at all. In other words, to use this parable, the dough does not rise on its own, but has something hidden inside that enables its rise.

For most people, as mentioned earlier, the idea that the creator of the world is a fundamentally different reality from the "fullness" or divine realm, is somewhat shocking. We are trained to think otherwise. That is why these insights are so astounding – they reveal a truth so provocative and radical that to understand it is to be changed. That is wakening, and what these insights are about.

From the Heart ...

That there is a hidden or esoteric meaning to most great spiritual insights is commonplace to me now. It took me a while to come to that truth, for my first inclination was to think that I was making something up, or seeing something that wasn't there. Very much like when I was a youngster having some "out of body" experiences: I was taken to the doctor to find out what was wrong with me. I immediately stopped having them.

To look for the hidden, or "concealed" truth of something is very important to spirituality. Everything is more than it appears to be, just like a behavior, while perhaps simple, has a very complex array of psychological factors beneath it. This ability to see underneath takes time to cultivate and nurture. That is why time for reflection, contemplation and meditation are so critical to spiritual development. I try to build that time into my schedule each and every day.

Insight 97

> Jesus said, "The kingdom of the father
> (and mother) is like a certain woman who was
> carrying a jar full of meal. While she was walking
> on the road, still some distance from home, the handle
> of the jar broke and the meal emptied out behind her
> on the road. She did not realize it, she had noticed
> no accident. When she reached her house, she
> set the jar down and found it empty."

From the Head ...

This parable, perhaps one of the most beautiful, describes very well the nature of modern depression and anxiety. Like people who are unaware that they are leaking the stuff of their being, they walk along a road mindless until they find themselves empty.

The sense of feeling empty is not a modern invention. We tend to think of concepts like alienation, depression and anxiety as belonging to the industrial and technological era, but they are existential in character, reflected here in this dramatic insight from almost 2,000 years ago. Our lives, Jesus is saying, are lived by accident. We become "broken jars," with nothing inside. Finding ourselves empty is a devastating affair. We are led to believe that being a good person and playing all the appropriate community roles, will result in a quality of understanding and sense of self that will give us wholeness. But, of course, it doesn't.

This story, like any good parable, lead us up to a question. What does the women do when she finds her jar broken and empty? It is like seeing that one's life is meaningless and without true substance.

What now? This is where the true drama unfolds, and so we are left to fill in the blank. The meal that was contained in the jar is the important thing. Perhaps the Spirit cannot escape its bondage until the jar is broken, until all our avenues of material reality are discovered to be simply a "broken jar." Many responses and interpretations are possible and necessary. That is the beauty of a parable such as this. It is timeless, and its truth transcends any one perspective.

From the Heart ...

Like most people, I spent years with my schedule full, and my "life" jam packed with stuff; busy, fruitful and well intentioned. I awoke one day to an "empty jar." Like in this story, it is a shocking conclusion. Imagine a women carrying a heavy jar for many miles. Upon her arrival home, she discovers that the contents had poured out, and what she thought would feed her was now just grains on the roadside. That is how I felt.

This insight is one of the most meaningful for me, and yet as I come to write about it, it is hard. Perhaps that is so because it touches so close to home – too close to where I sit. I imagine the women in story just sat and cried. That is all one can do at a moment of revelation like that. I certainly have had my share of tears. I imagine that she was angry and frustrated. I know those feeling well. I imagine that she wasn't sure what to do next, or how she would survive. I relate to that, too.

One might expect that Jesus would have said, as most people want to believe, that the "kingdom" is finding a full "jar," and in finding such, living happily ever after. That, of course, is fairy tale religiosity. The opposite is true: emptiness in the world is what is critical to eventual spiritual fullness. Sayings in the public Gospels also reflect this: "One must lose oneself in order to find oneself." And, "What does it profit a person to gain the whole world at the cost of his True Self?"

Authentic spirituality has a way of turning everything on its head. What we think is bad, turns out to be good, and vice versa. I think a parable such as this cannot be understood until it is lived. And, having lived it, I cannot find much more to say about it than this parable itself intimates. I am struck by the opening words of the Book of Ecclesiastes: "Emptiness, emptiness ... emptiness, all is empty." Those are the beginning words of Ecclesiastes. That is where it always begins, right where this parable leaves us.

Insight 98

> Jesus said, "The kingdom of the father
> (and mother) is like a certain man who wanted
> to kill a powerful man. In his own house he drew his
> sword and stuck it into the wall in order to find
> out whether his hand could carry through.
> Then he slew the powerful man."

From the Head ...

This parable is a link into later Gnostic redeemer mythology. Valentinus, the great Gnostic thinker of the second century, thought that the divine order had built a wall around itself as protection from the imbalance of the "created world" of the demiurge. To retrieve the spiritual light held captive by that created reality, a redeemer was sent to awaken the sleeping sparks that were lost in the noise and pressure of materiality. The wall had to be punched through as with a sword in order for the redeemer to traverse the barrier, also called the "the cross." In this way, the demiurge, here referred to as "the powerful man," would be slain (his hold on the lost Spirit destroyed), and the divine sparks retrieved back into the fullness. This is the esoteric meaning of this story, I believe; however it has practical applications as well.

It makes a great deal of sense to prepare for spiritual work by testing one's strength. We can easily become overwhelmed by the forces that we do battle with in our awakening. It takes courage and oftentimes sheer force to overcome the forces that impede us. This parable is of a violent nature, which Jesus expresses to point to the difficulty of spiritual awakening. It is never easy, and requires resolve and intentionality.

Another aspect of this parable is that the divine realm's presentation of itself in the world through the awakening of Spirit, is a violence to the order and system of materiality. It "overturns" or "breaks into" the small reality of physicality. It is not unusual for Jesus to speak of the kingdom in this way, but it is always shocking to those unaccustomed to the bluntness of these insights.

From the Heart . . .

There is no doubt in my mind that spiritual awakening does violence to the common order of things. It uproots, overturns, and disobeys the rules. The rules are: stay asleep, don't see and never talk about it. Most people abide by these rules religiously. Before one disobeys the rules in public, one must disobey the rules in private, that is, break their own rigidly controlled reality. Very much like the man in this story who practices killing the "powerful man" by sticking a sword through a wall just to see if he is strong enough to do it. We have to stick a sword through our inner walls before we can dynamite our social complexities.

My instinct was to act externally before I was prepared internally. Unlike the wise assassin in this story, I always wanted to run out and "fight the powerful man" before I knew whether I had the strength to do such a thing. And to be sure, even with all the inner practice in the world, we are never totally sure that we can do all that is necessary in our everyday world to bring about the change we need.

This story, like many of Jesus' stories, stands as a testimony of the dangers and pitfalls of spiritual awakening. To view yourself as an assassin wouldn't be the general kind of self-understanding that many would derive from spirituality; however, assassins we are in a sense. I've pinned this story up on my wall at times to help me focus on the seriousness of my awakening. Discipline, practice and focus, are all attributes the "assassin" must have, lest he become the assassinated.

Insight 99

> The disciples said to him, "Your brothers and
> your mother are standing outside. He said to them,
> "Those here who do the will of my father are my
> brothers and my mother. It is they who will
> enter the kingdom of the Spirit."

From the Head ...

This insight, and those that are like it in this collection as well as in the public Gospels, express several ideas. First, that there are those who stand "outside" the truth, and therefore make themselves unrelated to the truth. Secondly, that spiritual reality is much more important than flesh and blood. And finally, that the world makes a false division between human beings, thus hiding the truth "outside" within forms rather than as an internal recognition. Entering the kingdom is always an expression for spiritual awakening and discovering the "True Self."

Looking beyond the outward form of something is a common theme within Jesus' secret teachings. It is one of Jesus' most fundamental points: that we are lost within those forms, both physical and psychological, and that discovery of our true essence is critical to our being able to break free. This concept undoubtedly alienated Jesus from his earthly family, since it denied this most basic of physical authority, and placed Jesus outside all the societal laws designed to protect that structure. It is suggested in one public Gospel (Mark) that Jesus' family sought to have him "arrested" because he was "crazy." From the directness and tone of sayings like this one, I have no difficulty in believing the accuracy of that claim.

This insight harkens back to Jesus' claim that spiritual truth is an "easy yoke," as opposed to the heavy yoke of the world order. Family definitions and earthly history tie people into self-understandings and false reality forms that enslave the Spirit, and make soul work almost impossible. That is the intention of these forms, according to Jesus. So, to break their hold is of utmost importance.

From the Heart ...

I have already written of my struggle to overcome family and societal definitions. They are incredibly powerful. To come to the knowledge that the Spirit is your true family is an even more powerful recognition – for it releases you from all the psychological and material bondage that families usually bring with them. This is not to say that all families are bad – of course not. However, it is suggesting that the structuring of the system and the birth process itself are aspects of a false reality that cannot be taken too lightly. Jesus is quite clear on these points, and I have come to understand their depth only grudgingly.

As I view this now, I see all true life as a family – a fullness to which I beyond, and material process as a false reality that is something "outside" of my True Self. I think this is what Jesus was driving at in this insight. To be sure, it certainly brings the point to a focus. With all the talk of "traditional family values" thrown around in religious circles, this insight certainly makes a startling contrast. I find it interesting that so called conservatives and fundamentalists within Christianity see Jesus as a good family man. Not even the public Gospels point to that conclusion. We see what we need to see, I suppose.

Insight 100

They showed him a gold coin and said to him, "Caesar's men demand taxes from us." He said to them, "Give Caesar what belongs to Caesar, give God what belongs to God, and give me what is mine."

From the Head ...

This insight appears in the public Gospels as well. It has been used over and over to support any variety of political and economic positions. Normally this saying is interpreted as teaching the faithful to simply render unto Caesar what is Caesar's, and unto God what is God's. Ultimately the point is that everything belongs to God. If the image on the coin is the emperor's, whose image is the emperor made in? Why, God's, of course.

But this insight, unlike the public one, goes just a bit further. In the last sentence is the kicker. Jesus says, "and give me what is mine." Of interest here is that the emperor and God are really two aspects of the same reality. The coin has the emperor's image on it, and the emperor has God's image upon him. But Jesus separates himself out from that. He is saying, basically, that beyond all the images which belong to an ill-begotten world, is a quality that is indefinable and hidden, and that is what belongs to the world of the Spirit, here spoken of as "what is mine."

We should not miss that the public Gospels leave this end statement out. Since the orthodox church viewed all physical reality as created by the one true God, this insight expressed here would have to be abbreviated. Jesus, in these secret Gospels, uncontaminated by the orthodox control mechanisms, expresses something deeper and more insightful.

From the Heart . . .

Not all spiritual talk is truth. This is probably no great revelation to most folks, and it wasn't to me either, but it needs to be said here, and reinforced. To truly see, one has to look beyond the ordinary form into the depth of something. Take the saying of the coin and Caesar as written in the orthodox Bible. On the surface it seems fine – even beautiful. But look closer. When you place it alongside this secret teaching you begin to see the difference, which is at first subtle, and then huge. The orthodox folks left out the most important line which defined the entire insight. This kind of deliberate exclusion, it seems to me, is the basic problem with Christianity as it is practiced and viewed. The teachings of Jesus were replaced by teachings about Jesus, which in turn reframed his insights into just more of the same old dribble. Which is why I find the documents discovered at Nag Hammadi so intriguing and important. They give us a more pure insight as to the conflict between orthodox and Gnostic camps, and the emphasis which each side placed upon the insights of Jesus. Clearly, the Gospel of Thomas was intent on keeping talk about Jesus as much out of the focus as possible, and concentrated more on his insights. This was done, I think, to maintain clarity of message which, if history has demonstrated anything, is that Jesus' essential points were basically dissolved into a religious form he himself would have despised.

I find it interesting now, that I spent so many years trying to "reform" Christianity from inside the orthodox structure. It simply cannot be done that way. True reformation, if one can call it that, will take place as a movement that uses Christianity against itself to replace it with a form of Gnostic Christianity that is more basic to the truth of Jesus. I know that many people are beginning to catch on. That's a good sign.

Insight 101

> Jesus said, "Whoever does not hate his father
> and his mother as I do cannot become a disciple to me.
> And whoever does not love his father and his mother as I
> do cannot become a disciple to me. For my (earthly) mother
> is (an empty form), but my true mother gave me life."

From the Head ...

This insight, once again, expresses the emptiness of the dark world of forms. "Hating" one's earthly father and mother is not meant here to be a hostility about them, but rather an attitude toward the smallness and division caused by life in the world. We are defined by where we come from, and Jesus was quite clear that the world's false reality stemmed from its essential separation from the world of "fullness" and light. Every aspect of this world, therefore, was an aspect of that darkness – whether that is one's earthly family, race and color, or even political class distinctions. Defining oneself by family origin becomes an important item to be overcome, just as all earthly definitions are.

The last sentence is the lens through which this insight becomes clear. Earthly form is empty, "but my true mother gave me life." Jesus' true mother is the feminine quality of the divine fullness, sometimes referred to as Sophia in later Gnostic circles. This feminine aspect is the source of our divine spark – the Spirit that is enslaved to the world of false reality from which it must awaken.

This insight reflects a very common theme in Jesus' teachings. It strikes at the core of how we interpret and understand ourselves, and forces us into a new awareness of who we are, and where we come from. The awareness of one's True Self having originated from a reality beyond the scope of this world is the foundation of all authentic spirituality, and without this awareness all ideas of the Spirit become delusions from this world contrived to keep the Spirit at slumber. This realization is in part why Jesus chose to use the word "hate" to get our attention, for we generally are repelled from that which we hate, which is the goal here.

From the Heart ...

I do not "hate" my mother and father, at least not in any kind of normal definition of that term. I do recoil from family definition, and resist any attempt to confine my awakening into a box of material or psychological categories. I think that is what this insight suggests, and I am mindful about the power of what this teaching intends, which is to loosen us from our enslavement in the world.

Many teachings in this collection seem redundant, and they are. We learn best when we are told over and over again from many different angles. I remember having a person stop me after a church service where I had preached on a theme that I had preached on many times before. This person hugged me and told me how astounded they were by my teaching that morning, and how it affected them. I was aware, of course, that I had said nothing new, and had witnessed this same person many times listening to my words on exactly the same idea, not affected at all. Who knows why this particular morning awakened them? They were ready, was all I could come up with, which taught me the value of repeatedly teaching something over and over again.

The insight of one's True Self originating from beyond the universe of matter and energy is something that I think needs affirmation on a regular basis. The world has a way of making us feel that we are crazy to believe such a thing, particularly when all science and religion line up in opposition to such a revelation. Jesus was aware of the radical nature of this insight, and precisely because it is so radical and fundamental to spiritual awakening, he told it often and in a variety of ways. I'm glad he did.

Insight 102

> *Jesus said, "Woe to the Pharisees,*
> *for they are like a dog sleeping in the*
> *manger of oxen, for neither does he*
> *eat nor does he let the oxen eat."*

From the Head ...

Jesus sometimes made use of common sayings to derive a powerful meaning. This insight includes one such reference to a saying by Aesop (a dog sleeping in a manger of oxen does not eat, nor does he let the oxen eat).

The most powerful religious group in Jesus' time was the Pharisees, who we might liken to most Christian denominations of modern day. For Jesus the pharisaic perspective was a contra-force to the Spirit, for it had relegated spiritual truth to mere ritual and community convenience. The use of this Aesop saying was likely to be responded to by laughter, since to have it applied to a religious group would have been quite humorous, and a bit sacrilegious.

It's important for us to see the power of this kind of insight. A dog that does not eat, nor allows others to eat, soon creates starvation. Spiritual starvation is the result of profound ignorance, and when that ignorance becomes a religious force, it sustains and multiplies the starvation. Many people in our day and time will resonate with this insight, since it exposes the bankruptcy of religious ideas in the face of the human dilemma. We, too, may laugh a bit at the irony, and yet its meaning will not escape us.

From the Heart . . .

To suggest that most religious forms are spiritually bankrupt would be for many to state the obvious. As one friend put it, "Most preachers have nothing to say, but they try to say it well." How hungry we are for something of substance and meaning – not just "talk" about God, but an experience with the divine. Unfortunately, many people settle for a kind of emotionalism instead of authentic experience, since they are unwilling to do the hard inner work, and wish that spiritual truth would be just a simple matter of desire.

I have often struggled with my own spiritual hunger. Many times, whether I would like to admit this or not, I have been like the dog who would not eat, nor would I let others eat. I mean this primarily from an inner perspective. I see that aspects of myself would drive away other aspects of myself that needed spiritual enlightenment. Our inner world is dynamic and powerful, and not easily understood. There is a "pharisaic" part of me, like an ego control mechanism, that wants to stay in charge of focus and perspective, and fights against my willingness to move into other features of myself, with other awarenesses. Each of us must come to terms with this internal battle. Like all of Jesus' insights, they have an inside – outside meaning. The religious problems that I see in the world, are also a part of me. Until we come to terms with that, we never move beyond the convenience of our desires, into a world of mystery.

Insight 103

> *Jesus said, "Fortunate is the man who knows where the brigands will enter, so that he may get up, muster his domain, and arm himself before they invade."*

From the Head ...

Know your weakness. Each of us has weak points – drives that overwhelm us based on our experience of the world and our own psychological structure. To be true to one's self, one must know oneself, and guard against the weakness that invades that truth.

This insight is similar to one in the public Gospels where Jesus says that if a homeowner knows the time a thief would break into his home, he would not let him in. This is much like an alcoholic deciding to not go back to the bar, since it is a "slippery" place, and might cause him to drink again, even though there may be many old friends there. Each of us has our own particular "brigand" or "thief" that steals our truth, and places us in a malaise of issues.

Jesus often warned people to "be on guard." Spirituality requires discipline and attention, since the power of the world is great. In this battle, the most important "arms" are awareness, authentic knowledge, and love of the Spirit.

From the Heart ...

If insanity is the "doing of the same thing over and over again expecting different results," then we are all insane. If you look at existence from a spiritual perspective, the result is always the same –

death and decay. If you see life as a circle – seasons under the sun, or even as a line stretching into an unknown future – the conclusion remains unchanged. This pattern occurs externally and internally, and from a spiritual point of view, as I have said, it is truly insane.

What about me makes me want and need to "buy into" the system? What in me drives me toward the same patterns and desires, expecting as I always do, that an outcome will be different this time? Where is the weakness in my awareness, and how do I fortify myself against a breakdown in my focus and attention? These questions, and many others, must be addressed before I can become strong in my spiritual "domain."

In Insight 21, which has a similar thrust to this teaching, I wrote of how our consciousness is harvested by the world, "like a sickle thrown against the wheat." It requires us to stand guard, for the "brigand" or "thief" will come. That is an important notion to get, because the issue is not whether we will have our spiritual "domain" challenged, but where and when.

Insight 104

> *They said to Jesus, "Come, let us pray today and let us fast." Jesus said, "What is the sin that I have committed, or wherein have I been defeated? But when the bridegroom leaves the bridal chamber, then let them fast and pray."*

From the Head ...

Already Jesus had taught that fasting and praying were not essential to spiritual knowledge (Insight 6). What is essential is not lying to oneself, and not "doing what you hate." So, this insight tells us how difficult it is to break old patterns. Here the disciples are enacting a rote religious ritual without regard to their own inner knowledge. Jesus forces them to ask themselves why they would be doing such things. Speaking for the Spirit, as he often does, he asks, "What is the sin?" It forces the issue. The "sin" committed here by the disciples is the sin of unconsciousness and ignorance of self, which certainly cannot be overcome by enacting rituals unconsciously and without regard to self knowledge.

Also, again, we have Jesus referring to the bridegroom and bridal chamber. Since I dealt that notion elsewhere (Insight 75), I won't repeat it here. It will suffice to say when one is focused and involved with the Spirit (married to the Spirit!), the notions of fasting and prayer are irrelevant; it is only when that focus moves away from the Spirit that fasting and praying have any relevance at all.

From the Heart ...

I am reminded of a line from an old movie, "Harold and Maude," where Harold asks Maude: "Do you pray?" Maude thinks and says,

"No, I communicate." I think that was a Jesus-like answer. Beyond all the religious notions and ritualistic behaviors, is a very simple idea: communicate with the Spirit. In this "self communication" we discover our essence, and our origin, and the truth we need for our lives.

My "prayer" time is much more like contemplation I suppose. Perhaps authentic prayer is always a kind of listening, not begging or pleading. From that perspective, I pray a great deal. I think that is what Jesus meant in these rather bold teachings about prayer and fasting. We use these items as something separate from ourselves, as if they are pleasing to a God "out there" who is angry at us. To know the Spirit moves one beyond this need. God is not "out there," but in here. I do not need to "go to prayer," I become prayer itself.

These subtle things are so critical to spirituality. Maybe they aren't so subtle, they just feel that way to us who have a difficult time seeing what the true issues are. At any rate, those solitary times of sinking deeply into myself without talk and without agenda, those, it seems to me, are what prayer is all about – not some repeating of a proscribed set of words. Becoming solitary, then, is also the only real "fasting" necessary, since it is a fasting from the world and its agenda – which as we know, washes over us all the time.

Insight 105

> *Jesus said, "He who knows the father and the mother will be called the son of a harlot."*

From the Head ...

Tradition has it that Jesus was conceived by Mary before she was married. It is said that Jesus contended with this dilemma throughout his life, and that may well be. This insight appears to make reference to such a situation in Jesus' life, although given the nature of these insights, that certainly isn't all that it alludes to.

"He who knows the father and mother" refers to the spiritual knowing of divine origin. It's ironic that our divine origin, which supercedes all secondary realities such as our material birth, social station and the like, is viewed with such disregard. When one identifies with the Spirit it is given such little weigh in thinking, as to be likened to being a second class citizen. Although Jesus was particularly aware of this situation given the nature of his own birth, he nevertheless saw it as a metaphor for all awakened spirits living in a demented world that turns reality on its head.

Our spiritual father and mother is the only reality that matters. It is the material family and social force that directs the importance of "blood ties" that is the "harlot." That is what makes this insight so interesting and ironic. To make use of one's own situation as a way of teaching spiritual insight was a particular talent of Jesus'. I'm sure that those who had left family and friends to seek this higher spiritual reality appreciated this insight greatly, as did those who were the outcast of society – who, like Jesus, were looked down upon by others simply because of a contrived social belief. There is a simple brilliance in this insight, if we allow it to speak to us.

From the Heart ...

"It is easier for a camel to go through the eye of a needle than it is for a rich man to enter the kingdom of heaven." These words, from the public Gospels, ring in my ears as I read this insight. Those who are on the outside of societies most desirable can easily see the harshness of material reality. The social defenses do not work as well for them as they do for their more wealthy counterparts. Jesus calls this a "blessing," although it certainly doesn't feel as though it is a blessing.

Whenever I spend time with recovering alcoholics or drug addicts I am struck with a feeling that they have a certain "sensitivity" toward the world that is not found among the powerful and rich. Whether they make use of this "sensitivity" or not is another matter. Having been outcasts on the fringe of polite society, they can often see just how artificial it all is, and just how much it is merely our common defense against a harsh and uncaring world. This knowledge can be a powerful agent of awakening if guided in the right direction, or it can be an agent of continued sleep if viewed as a problem, instead of the first step toward a higher answer.

Jesus suggested that it was the "harlots" and the undesirables that point toward an answer to the human dilemma. Evil generally cloaks itself in respectability, and so it is not until we strip away the veneer of the polite clothing of the world that we are able to truly see. This simple insight pushes us to do just that.

Insight 106

> *Jesus said, "When you make the two one,*
> *you will become the sons of man, and when you say,*
> *'Mountain, move away,' it will move away."*

From the Head ...

The false division that is created by the world is once again empha-sized here. He makes use of his earlier teaching to "make the two one" (Insight 22) and couples it with "you will become the sons of man," which is a reference to spiritual awakening. Recall that in later Gnostic thinking, God's name is "Man," thus to identify oneself as a son (or daughter) of "Man" is to identify with divinity itself.

The "Mountain" that can be moved through this "becom(ing) the sons of man," is, of course, the world itself – a mountain that blocks vision into a deeper reality. To see beyond the mountain, one must move it or climb atop it.

Like all of Jesus' teachings in this collection, it also has a kind of cutting edge internally for us. It takes a great deal of work to get to the point of being able to say, "Mountain, move away," and actually have it move. This is why Jesus begins this insight with the statement "when you make the two one," which means that to move mountains there are prerequisites – hard inner work, and authentic self knowledge.

From the Heart ...

A friend once told me that this insight meant, "go get your shovel and get to work." There is some truth to that. To move a "reality mountain" requires standing in a place of knowledge. Simple faith that the mountain will move because of your faith is a ridiculous notion that the early church fostered to create a political and social structure. Which is why, after 2,000 years of "Christianity," no mountains have moved at all, just new ones created.

The issues we battle with in our spiritual awakening are perception, focus and reality formation. It is a constant issue, not one that is resolved with a doctrine or simple religious belief. I have "moved mountains," but getting to the point of even speaking to the mountain took great effort and insight on my part. Perhaps that is the central theme here – actually addressing the mountain – not getting it to move, at least not at first. One must first see the mountain before one can move it. Which is the most fundamental problem that most of us face, simply seeing that there is a mountain to move. If we see this "mountain" as mere obstacles to happiness or material well-being, we are not seeing the mountain at all. If we see this "mountain" as only psychological blocks or issues from childhood, or abuse or whatever else we encounter in our lives, we also miss the mark. The "mountain" is the common reality formation that we contend with everyday, whether we realize it or not. And we can be assured, this mountain "hides" so as not to be moved. I say hides, because that is exactly the nature of common reality – it "hides" in the everyday, which simply means that it is the everyday reality. Like comfortable clothing, we just naturally put it on because it "feels" comfortable. It's what we get use to. To overcome this "mountain" requires intentionality, focus and inner fluidity.

Once again, this insight drives to the core of Jesus' teachings. If you sit with it awhile, you will discover many aspects and layers to its simple directness. Don't take it too lightly, however. Let it work on you, I have, and it has made a great difference in my understanding and ability.

Insight 107

Jesus said, "The kingdom is like a shepherd who had a hundred sheep. One of them, the largest, went astray. He left the ninety-nine and looked for that one until he found it. When he had gone to such trouble, he said to the sheep, 'I care for you more than the ninety-nine.'"

From the Head ...

The good shepherd motif appears throughout Christian literature, perhaps because Jesus himself used it. Of course, the image of a shepherd was a familiar one in that day and time, and expresses a tenderness and nurturing that was not altogether common in religious thinking.

Beyond the obvious reference to caring for people who are outside the respectable social network, is the idea of the divine reality seeking that which has "fallen" into suffering and despair. The notion that the divine fullness seeks itself, that is, that part of itself that has become entangled in the darkness is central to understanding the shepherd imagery. After all, seen from this point of view, if a person breaks his arm, he tends to care for it more than the other parts of his body that are just fine. So, too, in this brief parable. The divine seeks the retrieval of its lost part, and thus cares for it more than the rest.

Insight such as this are always very loving and tender, and they are meant to be that way. Although much work is to be done with regard to awakening the Spirit, the awakening process is also a loving and tender one, since the result is wholeness and unity with the divine self. Imagine the divine fullness with many parts, and yet all one ultimate reality. Like a flock of sheep, if one aspect gets lost, it alarms the entirety. The shepherd goes to retrieve it.

In a way, each of us is required to be a shepherd, which simply means to care about the Spirit in whatever state of lostness it has fallen. Perhaps that is why this image has endured. It strikes at our need to be loved and cared for, even as we flounder in a dark and hostile world.

From the Heart ...

Becoming spiritually awake does not make one callous or hard hearted to the plight of others. While it is true that spirituality requires detachment, it does not require unloving apathy toward the Spirit wrapped tightly in the grip of the dark world that is yet unawakened. In fact, it intensifies the longing in a sense, because the awakened Spirit literally becomes aware of the fragmentation occurring in the world. Joy and sadness are often traveling companions in our journey here.

Although I feel a great distance between myself and many people in the world, I never feel so apart from them that I do not remember what it was like to not know who I was or where I came from. Perhaps being a "good shepherd" is knowing when to wait and watch, and when to speak up and act. An insight like this one makes me mindful of staying alert to the awakening Spirit of others.

Insight 108

> *Jesus said, "He who will drink from my mouth will become like me. I myself shall become he, and the things that are hidden will be revealed to him."*

From the Head ...

Hearing the truth changes us, if we are open and receptive. Once we truly hear, and allow the truth to pour into us, things become apparent that we could not have otherwise understood or recognized. This insight makes the powerful point that most orthodox perspectives tend to avoid, namely, that we each must become the truth. To be awakened to the truth of one's authentic self, one becomes the "Christ," and no longer identifies himself as he once did.

As always in these insights, there is an inside/outside dynamic. The truth of who we are is awakened by the truth of who someone else is. Jesus saw himself as a mirror, a kind of reflective presence that could awaken people if they received the image. I use the word awaken rather than learn, because we do not learn to be who we are, we simply awaken to the truth of who we are. In the knowledge of our true being, all authentic spiritual knowledge begins to unfold as a remembrance, not as something new or unique. "I myself shall become he, and the things that are hidden will be revealed to him," makes this exact point with precision.

From the Heart ...

We tend to deify someone who brings us a truth, but then as they disappoint us, as they always do, we destroy them because they let us down. The church has made the terrible mistake of deifying Jesus, and then glorifying his crucifixion as a sacrifice that will make a difference in our world. It doesn't and won't, because it can't. Why? Because that is the same thing we have always done since the beginning of history. We destroy our heroes, and then worship them so we don't have to become like them. The world system fosters this error, since it keeps us trapped in our invisible jail.

I think it is important that we hear and feel the intensity of this insight, if we truly are to awaken. We become the truth, we never worship it. Even in the time I have written about these insights I have come to see that more clearly. I remember writing that at one point "truth had become my religion." That is a mistake, which keeps truth separate and a part from who I am. This insight became clear in my thinking as I read it over and over again. As long as I worship something outside of my true essence, I never come to be the truth that I am. When I "drink from the mouth" of this teaching, and let it become me, truly those things "hidden are revealed." As usual, these insights in and of themselves have an awakening power, if I am able to receive them openly.

Insight 109

*Jesus said, "The kingdom is like a man who had
a hidden treasure in his field without knowing it. And
after he died, he left it to his son. The son did not know
about the treasure. He inherited the field and sold it.
And the one who bought it went plowing and
found the treasure. He began to lend money
at interest to whomever he wished."*

From the Head . . .

This parable, which is much like the pearl of great price that is found in the public Gospels, tells an interesting tale. The original owner of this field knew about the hidden treasure, but passed it along to his son without giving him knowledge of that treasure. The son, unwittingly, sells the field and thus gives away the treasure. Finally, the purchaser of the field discovers the treasure, and makes use of it by lending money, something that Jesus would never have approved of.

To understand this parable we must understand Jesus' perspective on the world and its origin. The original owner of the field is the creator God, who knows about the spiritual quality that he has trapped in his creation, but does not tell his son – who of course, is the unsuspecting human that he makes in "his image." The son just goes about his life metaphorically selling his hidden treasure to the world. And finally, the purchaser of the field – the world itself – lends the energy of the hidden treasure out "at interest," figurative language for paying a high and unnecessary price, to those unsuspecting souls who are just living their lives oblivious to what is happening.

When viewed from this context, this parable becomes a commentary on the human dilemma. There is something hidden that is being inappropriately used, and knowledge of this situation is paramount to its unraveling. It is no mistake that this insight comes on the heels of the previous one concerning hidden things being revealed if one drinks from the mouth of truth. I would imagine that this insight, although somewhat esoteric in nature, was clearly seen by those awake enough to view its essence, and close to Jesus' heart and mind on the subject of our need for liberation.

From the Heart ...

As my awakening has deepened, I have discovered greater and more profound meaning in parables such as this one. What better way to show us how difficult our situation is than to tell a story like this one. On the surface we might say, "How lucky for the new land owner who discovered the treasure! What's wrong with lending it out at interest?" But when you view this from a spiritual perspective, it becomes much clearer as to the real point. How inappropriately our spiritual essence is used by the world. So much so, that our essence is used to perpetuate our own enslavement.

This is not an easy thing to understand, and most of us would not want it to be true. But it is, and all we need do is open our eyes and see the truth. Spiritual life is misused and enslaved in objects, symbols, forces and ideas that lead back to its own enslavement. A parable like this one helps keep us focused and clear headed, if we use it to keep us awake.

Insight 110

> Jesus said, "Whoever finds the world and becomes rich, let him renounce the world."

From the Head ...

Becoming "rich" is a metaphor for having become enmeshed in the world organizational system – both social and biological. That is to say, ascribing a kind of ultimacy to it that fosters denial of the alien Spirit. It is easy to become so wrapped up in survival that one forgets to attend to the Spirit, which according to later Gnostic thought was an intentional situation developed by the creator God to keep humankind asleep and intoxicated with the world. Here Jesus is referring to a common theme in his teachings – renunciation of the world in favor of a higher reality: the world of the Spirit.

So predominant is this theme that Jesus refers to it six times in this collection (Insights 21, 27, 56, 80, 110 & 111). While many scholars have discarded this type of sayings as authentic Jesus teachings because they do not appear directly in the public Gospels, they were most likely – as we see here – central to his private and personal teachings to those closest to him. After all, it is this type of teaching that made Jesus controversial and politically/religiously unacceptable. To simply teach of love and God's love of the poor and downtrodden was a common theme throughout Judaism. It was not until the teachings of this variety, namely Jesus direct referencing of another reality beyond the boundaries of this world, that Jesus' conflict with the rulers began in earnest. It is very possible that many of these sayings were deliberately left out of the public Gospels because they do not lend themselves well to the creation of political and economic structures of church organization.

From the Heart . . .

As I have written earlier at various places, it was a difficult process for me to let go of my "riches" with the world system. To step away from definitional realities, common and ordinary life patterns and all the psychological and social forces that keep that in place, is never an easy thing. The most difficult part is the inner battle, which rages between taught reality and revealed reality. I think most of us have gone through this kind of conflict, but decide that our inner revelational material coming from an awakening Spirit is nothing but social rebelliousness and wishful thinking. So, consequently, we turn away from the revealed reality and attach to the taught reality of the world system. This is what Jesus called being "rich" with the world. It's another way of saying being intoxicated or "over stuffed" with the world's idea of itself – much like a person's ego sees itself as the only reality of the individual.

This situation is one that I am constantly made aware of inside myself and in my contact with others. Being aware of how contaminating the world is to the Spirit, I frequently visualize myself being "washed" by light as a way of symbolizing my freedom from it. Perhaps this was what baptism meant to the earliest Christians, and most especially the Gnostics, but I think it is a daily affair not a one-time gesture. The form matters much less than does the practice of awareness. Unfortunately, most religious organizations, since they are designed to self-perpetuate, place more emphasis on the form than on the content and meaning.

Insight 111

> *Jesus said, "The heavens and the earth will roll up in your presence, and whoever is living from the living one will not see death." Does not Jesus say, "Whoever finds himself is superior to the world?"*

From the Head ...

This insight is a little different from the rest, in that it contains a statement by Thomas for emphasis. He adds: "Does not Jesus say," and then attaches another one of Jesus' insights as a qualifier (Insight 56). To have "heaven and earth roll up in your presence" is an awesome vision, and it strips away any ascribed ultimacy to our notions of earthly life and ordinary perceptions of heaven. No reference is made to a new heaven and earth being created in the aftermath, since spiritual reality will have replaced the need and desire for such a thing to have occur.

The idea of "not see(ing) death," appears several times in this collection and has a special import. Since death is a part of the world system, it stands to reason that finding the spiritual reality outside of that system one would not "see death" there. Thus, the finding of one's True Self is essentially what it means to "live from the living one."

From the Heart ...

"Living from the living one," is the phrase that I found most interesting in this insight. Of course, I understand that Jesus is referring to the Spirit – since it has life and all else is but a shadow of that life. It also reminded me of the unity of the Spirit that is so essential in Jesus' teachings in this collection. Living from the living *one*, invites me to re-frame my thinking, actions and even my feelings, toward this spiritual reality that is my True Self.

Recently I heard the "mantra" of the world order that says, "Death is a part of life." What hogwash. Death is not a part of life, since by definition it is not life. While it is true that physical life feeds off death, and sustains physical life until it becomes part of the food chain itself, to revere death as a wholesome part of a harmonious system is a great lie of the world that keeps us distracted from what we know inside ourselves to be true. It is how we explain away our pain and suffering, and try to make it rational and sensible in an alien and hostile world. To blame death and decay on the "sinful nature" of human beings, as religious doctrine often does, is so incredibly ridiculous as to be an aspect of evil itself. It is like blaming a person for getting muddy after having pushed them into a mud pit.

I understand death to be part of a limited reality that does not control or define who I am. I do not "see" it as ultimate, or having a claim on my being. Because I know this to be true, heaven and earth are rolled up, and I feel a sense of freedom to simply walk through life living from that knowledge. I think that is what Jesus means here, and why Thomas wanted to emphasize it with his piggy backing it to another one of Jesus' insights regarding becoming "superior" to the world. Instead of chanting the world's mantra of "death is a part of life," I prefer to "live from the living one."

Insight 112

> Jesus said, "Woe to the flesh that depends on the soul; woe to the soul that depends on the flesh."

From the Head ...

This insight, very much like Insight 87, suggests the terrible situation we find ourselves in, and the necessary work that needs to be done in order to achieve liberation. The soul is that in between aspect of our being that can turn either way – toward the Spirit, or toward the flesh. The flesh is doomed no matter what course it takes, and since it does depend of the soul for mindful movement in the world, the first part of this insight is just a statement of fact, and the real action is with the second part. The question that always confronts us is whether we have attached to the materiality of the world, or whether our soul has moved beyond it into the world of the Spirit.

"Soul work," as I have mentioned before, is always hard work. It requires knowledge from both the spiritual and material side of our being. The Spirit points to a reality indefinable by worldly standards, and the material world rubs our noses in the suffering of its blind process. Being caught between these two forces feels very much like a battle, and is, as we have seen throughout history, good material for literature and storytelling.

This insight is a re-emphasis of something that Jesus held to be of utmost importance. It is said in a variety of ways, and often. Perhaps Jesus meant this insight to be like an alarm clock to awaken a sleeping part of us – it goes off periodically just in case we are caught napping.

From the Heart ...

This insight forced me to think about the nature of the soul. I decided after having written the first part of this insight from my head, that I would need to take a walk and let it sink into my heart so I could write this last part. What I found in my heart was a clear sense of my soul being a quality that is not exactly the same as my mind, or my ego or anything that I could easily identify, but that it was the repository of all those items and much more. Exactly as the insight suggests, the question is whether this "quality" is attached to my "flesh" or beyond it to the world of the Spirit. For me, I felt immediately that my soul was very identified with my Spirit at this point, and that writing about these insights had solidified that movement. How did I know this? I asked myself that question as well. The only answer I could attain was that it was known spiritually and revealed as such. My mind, of course, not being identical with my soul, is often occupied by material affairs, as it must be. But my soul looks to the Spirit for its strength and sense of purpose and identity, as Jesus suggested was the only way to seek liberation.

My sense is that many people who read this book will find that these insights themselves will move them. I certainly have. I will write more about that in an "Afterwards" section, but an insight like this one certainly makes me think about it. Awareness and awakening are two fundamentals to "soul work," that need to be mentioned repeatedly in any spiritual discipline. Jesus does that, and Thomas as a worthy disciple made it a point to write it down several times for our study.

Insight 113

> *His disciples said to him, "When will the kingdom come?"*
> *Jesus said, "It will not come by waiting for it. It will not*
> *be a matter of saying 'here it is' or 'there it is.' Rather,*
> *the kingdom of the father and mother is spread*
> *out upon the earth, and men do not see it."*

From the Head ...

This insight, which has several parallels in the public Gospels and also in this collection, restates Jesus' view of a spiritual reality that is already present within us – here mentioned as being "spread out upon the earth" – that cannot be seen from ordinary reality perspectives. That "men do not see it" is not viewed as a matter of lacking belief so much as simply being asleep to the truth of who they are. For after all, many people believe that some kind of religious event is historically coming, and yet do not realize their own true nature.

Most modern scholarship today is in agreement that sayings like this are authentic Jesus teachings, and I agree. That Jesus somehow expected an earthly kingdom seems to be the issue, but it is clear from the sayings themselves that he does not. Quite the contrary, the kingdom of the father and mother is not a better or revised material existence, but rather a world of light which defies definition from physical and energy concepts. It is already "spread out upon the earth," because it is the Spirit itself, and since humankind is spread out over the earth, so is the kingdom.

If you read this insight alongside of Insight 17 where Jesus says that he will give us "what no eye has ever seen," you come to realize the depth of this teaching. Eyes of flesh and blood cannot see the kingdom, nor can anything that is of "this world." To see the kingdom one must see with the eyes of the Spirit. Since Jesus frequently speaks of himself as the Spirit speaking to us, it stands to reason that he would also say that he is revealing a special kind of knowledge – spiritual knowledge that he calls "the kingdom."

It is brilliant imagery to say that something is spread out over everything and yet cannot be seen. Like a riddle, it unfolds before us, and tickles our imagination. This teaching is meant to awaken us, as so many of Jesus' sayings are. It reaches inside of us and shakes our very being in hopes of jarring the Spirit from its sleep.

From the Heart ...

What fascinates me about the Jesus' insights is not only the obvious spiritual value of them, but also the beautiful way in which they are phrased. That a spiritual reality is "spread out upon the earth" and yet cannot be seen, has a kind of compelling and beckoning ring to it. It was always sayings like this one that captured my imagination, and made me think. Now, of course, I see what Jesus said could not be seen, and that makes this kind of insight all the more moving and wonderful. I see that it, in and of itself, has an awakening vibration to it, for lack of a better way of putting it, and literally does something to our insides when we read it.

But another thing that this insight calls my attention to is the fact that people do not see it, and when they do, it forces them to be at odds with a blind world that guides people blindly. You can talk and argue until you are blue in the face, but until a person is awakened they will not see it, and that is the sad fact of the matter. How someone awakens is a mystery. It happens differently for each of us, I suppose, so there is no formula or ritual to perform. But I have a sense that teachings like these are not just good spiritual language, but have a kind of force to them that truly taps into a spiritual level and begins the work of awakening. That certainly has been true for me.

Insight 114

Simon Peter said to them, "Let Mary leave us, for women are not worthy of life." Jesus said, "I myself shall lead her in order to make her male, so that she too may become a living spirit resembling you males. For every women who will make herself male will enter the kingdom of heaven."

From the Head ...

At first reading this insight might appear sexist and typical of first century thinking about women, but that is not at all the case. Peter, being rather dull witted, is alarmed that Jesus has taken Mary as one of his disciples – something the orthodox church has denied much to its own detriment, and asks that she be dismissed from their presence. Jesus, rather humorously I think, tells him that he himself will "make her male" so Peter can overcome his bias.

But this insight is more than that, of course. It echoes previous insights where Jesus tells us that it is important to do away with distinctions, whether they are gender oriented, class related or racial. And, this is not only true on the outside of us – in our social-political environment – but also on the inside of us as well, where work needs to be done to balance our internal perspectives and energies so we might be able to see the kingdom that Jesus says is "spread out upon the earth."

This insight drives to the heart of the dark training that occurs in our social world that reflects the biological training that occurs in the natural world. The strong survive, and the weak die – that is the lesson. Men are stronger, at least in some physical ways, and that strength has been used to justify enslavement and abuse of women from the beginning of time. Here Jesus is attempting to change thought patterns that have been drummed into men all their lives. Peter, who is so revered in the orthodox church as "the rock," is not held in such high esteem in the private teachings. It is Mary, the "apostle's apostle" who truly understands her beloved Jesus' teachings, and has a special insight into their meaning. (I highly recommend reading *The Gospel of Mary*, which to my mind is a brilliant work. Unfortunately, several sections are missing, but nevertheless it remains a highly informative piece of literature.)

This is where this collection ends. As well it should. We are left to ponder what it takes to break our earthly reality, and move into the world of the Spirit. Peter was forced to confront his small-mindedness and his brainwashing. So are we all.

From the Heart ...

I laughed and laughed when I read this insight just now. When I first read it years ago, I was shocked to see it here among these other "enlightened" thoughts. I thought, this doesn't belong here – it's so sexist and brutal. But as I see it now, it most certainly does belong here, and needs to be here just because it is sexist and brutal. Peter is every man – the ordinary world that hears, but does not listen, watches but does not see. And Mary, who does not say a word, must know that she knows more than Peter probably will ever let himself know. Strange isn't it, that this ignorance and stupidity continues in the priesthood among the Catholics, and in the inability of many Protestant denominations to allow women into the ministry. As a friend once said, "The more things change, the more they stay the same."

As for the internal meaning of this insight, I think Carl Jung and other noted psychologists have done significant work in uncovering how out of balance with these sexual energies we have become, and what it takes to overcome them. After all, the Spirit does not have a gender like our physical bodies do. While there is a sexuality to the Spirit world, it does not foster the division and hurtfulness that the material matrix so obviously does.

That this insight should be the last one seems to me to be fitting somehow. As I said above in the "From the Head" section, it leaves us with a question about ourselves I think. It is very difficult to overcome our conditioning to get fluid enough to truly see with the eyes of the Spirit. Peter, perhaps, had sat there and listened to Jesus many times, but when it came right down to it, he just didn't get it. Maybe it was Mary who finally helped him overcome his earthly insanity. I like to think that she did.

Afterwards

"Whoever findings the meaning of these sayings will not experience death." This is how this collection of insights begins. Did Jesus think that these sayings, in and of themselves, would begin an inner change in the individual that would ultimately lead to an awakening that would liberate him from the bondage of suffering that this world is? Well, whatever Jesus thought about them, they certainly have a power. One cannot live with these insights for a period of time and not have them radically affect the way that you feel, think and move in the world.

I have read this Gospel many times now, and have focused on each insight to give it time to sink in and touch my deepest part. What occurred has been nothing short of incredible, for truly I feel a sense of my own change, and a sense that I will never be the same again. Somehow they moved me from identifying with an "I" that I thought I was, to an "I" that I now understand to be who I truly am. Within this new understanding, death is no longer a factor, since it stands outside of the truth of my essential being. Not by faith, nor belief in a doctrine or historical event, but through simply knowing who I am has caused this change, exactly as Jesus said it would.

When I began this book, I separated each insight into reactions from my head and from my heart. I wanted to be free to be more intellectual in the "head" part, and more "feeling and emotional" in the second. What I found, however, was that neither part held the answer, but something was beyond them both that was affecting me and stripping layers away, that I could not fully understand with either of those parts of my existence. I suppose that I could re-write this book and do it differently now, but I will let it stand as a visible process.

Printed in the United States
1059800005B